Engaging God's Word

Hebrews

Engage Bible Studies
Tools That Transform

Engage Bible Studies

an imprint of

COMMUNITY
BIBLE STUDY

Engaging God's Word: Hebrews
Copyright © 2012 by Community Bible Study. All rights reserved.
ISBN 978-1-62194-006-7

Published by Community Bible Study
790 Stout Road
Colorado Springs, CO 80921-3802
1-800-826-4181
www.communitybiblestudy.org

Printed in the United States of America.

Contents

Introduction

Welcome to the life-changing adventure of engaging with God's Word! Whether this is the first time you've opened a Bible or you've studied the Scriptures all your life, good things are in store for you. Studying the Bible is unlike any other kind of study you have ever done. That's because the Word of God is *"living and active"* (Hebrews 4:12) and transcends time and cultures. The earth and heavens as we know them will one day pass away, but God's Word never will (Mark 13:31). It's as relevant to your life today as it was to the people who wrote it down centuries ago. And the fact that God's Word is living and active means that reading God's Word is always meant to be a personal experience. God's Word is not just dead words on a page—it is page after page of living, powerful words—so get ready, because the time you spend studying the Bible in this *Engaging God's Word* course will be life-transforming!

Why Study the Bible?

Some Christians read the Bible because they know they're supposed to. It's a good thing to do, and God expects it. And all that's true! However, there are many additional reasons to study God's Word. Here are just some of them.

We get to know God through His Word. Our God is a relational God who knows us and wants us to know Him. The Scriptures, which He authored, reveal much about Him: how He thinks and feels, what His purposes are, what He thinks about us, how He views the world He made, what He has planned for the future. The Bible shows us God's many attributes—His kindness, goodness, justice, love, faithfulness, mercy, compassion, creativity, redemption, sovereignty, and so on. As we get to know Him through His Word, we come to love and trust Him.

God speaks to us through His Word. One of the primary ways God
speaks to us is through His written Word. Don't be surprised if, as you
read the Bible, certain parts nearly jump off the page at you, almost
as if they'd been written with you in mind. God is the Author of this
incredible book, so that's not just possible, it's likely! Whether it is
to find comfort, warning, correction, teaching, or guidance, always
approach God's Word with your spiritual ears open (Isaiah 55:3)
because God, your loving heavenly Father, has things He wants to say
to you.

God's Word brings life. Just about everyone wants to learn the secret
to "the good life." And the good news is, that secret is found in God's
Word. Don't think of the Bible as a bunch of rules. Viewing it with that
mindset is a distortion. God gave us His Word because as our Creator
and the Creator of the universe, He alone knows how life was meant to
work. He knows that love makes us happier than hate, that generosity
brings more joy than greed, and that integrity allows us to rest more
peacefully at night than deception does. God's ways are not always
"easiest" but they are the way to life. As the Psalmist says, *"If Your law
had not been my delight, I would have perished in my affliction. I will never
forget Your precepts, for by them You have given me life"* (Psalm 119:92-93).

God's Word offers stability in an unstable world. Truth is
an ever-changing negotiable for many people in our culture
today. But building your life on constantly changing "truth" is
like building your house on shifting sand. God's Word, like God
Himself, never changes. What He says was true yesterday, is true
today, and will still be true a billion years from now. Jesus said,
*"Everyone then who hears these words of Mine and does them will be
like a wise man who built his house on the rock"* (Matthew 7:24).

God's Word helps us to pray effectively. When we read God's Word
and get to know what He is really like, we understand better how to
pray. God answers prayers that are according to His will. We discover
His will by reading the Bible. First John 5:14-15 tells us that *"this is
the confidence that we have toward Him, that if we ask anything according
to His will He hears us. And if we know that He hears us in whatever we
ask, we know that we have the requests that we have asked of Him."*

How to Get the Most
out of *Engaging God's Word*

Each *Engaging God's Word* study contains key elements that have
been carefully designed to help you get the most out of your time in
God's Word. Slightly modified for your study-at-home success, this
approach is very similar to the tried-and-proven Bible study method that
Community Bible Study has used with thousands of men, women, and
children across the United States and around the world for nearly 40
years. There are some basic things you can expect to find in each course
in this series.

- ❖ Lesson 1 provides an overview of the Bible book (or books) you
  will study and questions to help you focus, anticipate, and pray
  about what you will be learning.

- ❖ Every lesson contains questions to answer on your own,
  commentary that reviews and clarifies the passage, and three
  special sections called "Apply what you have learned," "Think
  about" and "Personalize this lesson."

- ❖ Some lessons contain memory verse suggestions.

Whether you plan to use *Engaging God's Word* on your own or with a
group, here are some suggestions that will help you enjoy and receive the
most benefit from your study.

Spread out each lesson over several days. Your *Engaging God's Word*
lessons were designed to take a week to complete. Spreading out your
study rather than doing it all at once allows time for the things God is
teaching you to sink in and for you to practice applying them.

Pray each time you read God's Word. The Bible is a book unlike any
other because God Himself inspired it. The same Spirit who inspired
the human authors who wrote it will help you to understand and apply
it if you ask Him to. So make it a practice to ask Him to make His Word
come alive to you every time you read it.

Read the whole passage covered in the lesson. Before plunging into the questions, take time to read the specific chapter or verses that will be covered in that lesson. Doing this will give you important context for the whole lesson. Reading the Bible in context is an important principle in interpreting it accurately.

Begin learning the memory verse. Learning Scripture by heart requires discipline, but the rewards far outweigh the effort. Memorizing a verse allows you to recall it whenever you need it—for personal encouragement and direction, or to share with someone else. Consider writing the verse on a sticky note or index card that you can post where you will see it often or carry with you to review during the day. Reading and re-reading the verse often—out loud when possible—is a simple way to commit it to memory.

Re-read the passage for each section of questions. Each lesson is divided into sections so that you study one small part of Scripture at a time. Before attempting to answer the questions, review the verses that the questions will cover.

Answer the questions without consulting the Commentary or other reference materials. There is great joy in having the Holy Spirit teach you God's Word on your own, without the help of outside resources. Don't cheat yourself of the delight of discovery by reading the Commentary prematurely. Wait until after you've completed the lesson.

Repeat the process for all the question sections.

Prayerfully consider the "Apply what you have learned," marked with the 📌 push pin symbol. The vision of Community Bible Study is not to just gain knowledge about the Bible, but to be transformed by it. For this reason, each set of questions closes with a section that encourages you to apply what you are learning. Usually this section involves action—something for you to do. As you practice these suggestions, your life will change.

Read the Commentary. *Engaging God's Word* commentaries are written by theologians whose goal is to help you understand the context of what you are studying as it relates to the rest of Scripture, God's character, and what the passage means for your life. Of necessity, the commentaries include the author's interpretations. While interesting and helpful, keep in mind that the Commentary is simply one person's understanding of what these passages mean. Other godly men and women have views that are also worth considering.

Pause to contemplate each "Think about" section, marked with the notepad symbol. These features, embedded in the Commentary, offer a place to pause and consider some of the principles being brought out by the text. They provide excellent ideas to journal about or to discuss with other believers, especially those doing the study with you.

Jot down insights or prayer points from the "Personalize this lesson" marked with the ☑ check box symbol. While the "Apply what you have learned" section focuses on doing, the "Personalize this lesson" section focuses on becoming. Spiritual transformation is not just about doing right things and refraining from doing wrong things—it is about changing from the inside out. To be transformed means letting God change our hearts so that our attitudes, emotions, desires, reactions, and goals are increasingly like Jesus'. Often this section will discuss something that you cannot do in your own strength—so your response will usually be something to pray about. Remember that becoming more Christ-like is not just a matter of trying harder—it requires God's empowerment.

Lesson 1

Fulfillment in Jesus
Hebrews 1:1-4

When life is hard, it's especially essential to have a solid foundation. The book of Hebrews was written to a group of Christians who were facing difficult times. They needed the reassurance that what, and even more importantly, who, they believed in was absolutely trustworthy. And they needed encouragement that would help them to persevere in persecution. In his attempt to provide for these needs, the unidentified author of Hebrews presents a water-tight defense of Jesus Christ, in whom they have believed, along with examples, exhortation, and encouragement to stay in the race. Some themes of Hebrews include:

- ❖ Jesus is 100-percent God and 100-percent man.
- ❖ Jesus is both eternal sacrifice and eternal High Priest, atoning for the sins of men and women and interceding for them before God.
- ❖ Jesus is better than angels, Moses, the Law, and the earthly sacrificial system.
- ❖ God offers rest to those who listen to His voice and believe Him.
- ❖ Jesus is our example of enduring faith in the midst of opposition and suffering.
- ❖ Faith is essential to pleasing God and living the Christian life successfully.
- ❖ God's promises are absolutely trustworthy; some are realized in this life, others only in the consummation of the Kingdom of God.
- ❖ God calls us to endure under trial—and to encourage fellow believers also to persevere.

1. How does the importance of enduring under trial connect with
    your current circumstances?

    _____

    _____

    _____

2. How does your faith in Jesus provide practical encouragement
    and assistance in the difficulties you face?

    _____

    _____

    _____

3. On a scale from one to five, how would you describe your faith?
    Why would you describe it that way?

    _____

    _____

    _____

4. As we study God's Word, our goal is to be transformed by it. As you
    think about the truths you will be studying in this course, which
    one seems most important for your spiritual growth right now?

    _____

    _____

    _____

*If you are doing this study with a group, take time to pray for one another
about your answers to question 4. Ask God to reveal truth to you as you study
about this, and even more importantly, to make you more like Jesus as a result.
If you are studying by yourself, write your prayer in the blank space below.*

Lesson 1 Commentary

Fulfillment in Jesus
Hebrews 1:1-4

While technically a letter, the book of Hebrews reads like a well-crafted sermon. The author uses the Old Testament to prove the greatness and superiority of Jesus over all who had gone before. Salvation had been foreshadowed in an imperfect priestly system, but now is fulfilled in the one eternal High Priest, Jesus, whose offering of Himself meets all requirements for humanity's salvation.

This book establishes that the Mosaic system is no longer binding upon New Testament believers. We now have a new standing before God because Christ has made obsolete the law of sacrifice and ritual by His blood atonement. Yet Hebrews does not negate the Old Testament; rather it sums up its Law because the Law finds its fulfillment in the finished work of the Son of God. The Old and New Testaments are inseparably linked as God's revelation of Himself.

The author has two purposes: to instruct and challenge. The goal of instruction is to prove that Jesus is God's perfect revelation of salvation. The challenge focuses on (1) an emphasis on God's Word; (2) a call to perseverance; and (3) a call to obedience in faith. The writer intends to show from Scripture that Jesus is the uniquely begotten Son of God, yet a truly human mediator. By offering His life, He paid the death penalty due all people.

The term *Hebrews* is not used in this letter. The unnamed author is writing to a community of believers he cares about. They are likely Jewish Christians who have suffered some persecution and their spiritual progress has been arrested. Hebrews was probably written between AD 60 and 70. Due to a lack of evidence, we must accept uncertainties about Hebrew's author, audience, and origin.

The beginning of Hebrews contains no greeting typically associated
with a letter. The author describes the writing as a *"word of exhortation"*
(Hebrews 13:22). Although the beginning reads more like a sermon,
the writing ends like a letter, with brief personal news, greetings, and
benedictions.

The author begins by explaining the uniqueness and finality of God's
revelation through His Son, Jesus Christ. This revelation was given
first to the Jewish forefathers through the prophets, and finally, *"to us
by His Son"* (1:2). With the coming of the Son, a new era has begun.
The old era, marked by incompleteness and promise, is fulfilled by the
life and work of Jesus. This new era is characterized by permanence,
completeness, and finality. The opening verses state the theme of
Hebrews: Christ's revelation is superior to all that had come before His
arrival.

Being *"appointed the heir of all things"* (1:2) cannot mean that the Son
has been given something He lacked, or that ownership has passed to
Him from the Father. The universe has always belonged to the Son,
because through Him all created existence came into being. God
the Son, by His choice to identify and save, inherited the right to be
worshiped in heaven and on earth. His heirship is connected to His work
of redemption. In the beginning the Son is Creator, and in the end He
inherits His creation. Hebrews 1:2 establishes the exclusiveness of the
Son. Christians are also called children and heirs of God, but solely by
virtue of their incorporation by faith into the only begotten Son.

Christ pre-existed all created things and co-existed with the Father from
the beginning. *"He is the radiance of the glory of God and the exact imprint
of His nature"* (1:3). Jesus Christ, though born of a woman and truly
human, is of the same order of existence as God—He is, in fact, God.
His radiance reminds us of the *shekinah* glory, which signified God's
presence, and also of the glory seen at His Transfiguration.

As the radiance reveals the light, so the Son reveals the Father. The
Greek word translated *"exact imprint"* suggests an engraving on a coin;
the Greek word translated *"nature"* denotes the very substance of God.
The substance or essence of God is in Christ.

The Son does not merely resemble certain aspects of His Father; He is
the exact representation of His essence. The Son Himself said, *"Whoever*

has seen Me has seen the Father" (John 14:9). The author asserts that Jesus *"upholds the universe by the word of His power"* (1:3). Just as the universe was called into existence by the Father's word, so it is actualized and sustained by the utterance of His Son. The one in whom all things were created is also the one in whom *"all things hold together"* (Colossians 1:17).

Think about how Scripture shows that the Father, Son, and Holy Spirit are one in essence, thus one in purpose. The church has held to the truth that Jesus Christ is fully God and fully man, one with the Father in purpose and personality. Jesus prayed that we would be in the Father and in Him, as the Father is in the Son and the Son is in the Father. God wants us to be one with Him in purpose and behavior. Just as the Son was strengthened by doing His Father's will, so He desires that we submit ourselves to Him so that His will becomes ours. Then we can say with Jesus, *"I can do nothing on My own"* (John 5:30), and with Paul, *"I can do all things through Him who strengthens me"* (Philippians 4:13).

The theme of Jesus as our High Priest is evident in the last sentence of verse 3. By providing purification for sins, the Son accomplished something no other representative could do. He then *"sat down,"* demonstrating that the work of purification was complete. Seated at God's right hand—a position of honor and authority—Christ now rules with God.

The Son, who for our redemption humbled Himself for a time to a position lower than that of the angels, has been exalted by His ascension to a position higher than theirs. The Son's eternal character is not suddenly superior, but the *work* of the Son is proven incomparable. The *"name"* that distinguishes Christ from the angels and elevates Him above them is that of *Son*.

Personalize this lesson.

✓ Is change hard for you? It is for many people. Change often means that our comfortable status quo is interrupted. Our familiar routines, lifestyles and ways of relating to others are disrupted. We don't know what to expect anymore. The author of Hebrews challenged his readers to change. He asked them to let go of tradition and embrace the freedom and rest—and possible hardship— that come from making Jesus supreme in their personal lives and corporate gatherings. Although change would obviously be for their good, it was probably pretty uncomfortable. Similarly, as you read this book, God may also challenge you to change. Are you ready? Do you trust Him enough to follow His lead, even if it takes you out of your comfort zone? Ask Him to increase your faith so you will not only learn important truth from Hebrews, but so that your life will be transformed by that truth.

The Superiority of Christ
Hebrews 1:1–2:9

Memorize God's Word: Hebrews 1:1-2.

❖ Hebrews 1:5-7—The Question

1. The author of Hebrews quotes from Psalm 2. What does that tell you about how the early church viewed the Old Testament?

   _____

   _____

   _____

2. From Acts 13:32-37, what facts are given that are not present in Hebrews 1:5-7?

   _____

   _____

   _____

   _____

3. From the following Scripture passages, how did God use angels in Old Testament history?

   a. Genesis 19:1-17 _____

   _____

   _____

   b. Exodus 23:20-23 _____

   _____

   _____

    c.   Daniel 8:15-19 _____

_____

_____

4.   What is the relationship between the angels and Christ?

_____

_____

_____

_____

❖ Hebrews 1:8-12—The Argument Set Forth

5.   List the characteristics and works of Christ that you find in these verses.

_____

_____

_____

_____

_____

_____

6.   Verses 10-12 make a comparison. How would you explain these verses to someone unfamiliar with Scripture?

_____

_____

_____

_____

_____

❖ Hebrews 1:13–2:4—The Argument's Conclusion

7.   What is one of the tasks of angels, according to 1:14?

_____

_____

8. a. Chapter 1 does not discredit angels; it does exalt the Son. On that basis, what significant truth is implied in Hebrews 2:1-3?

_____

_____

   b. Suggest how the truth of Hebrews 2:1 can be applied throughout your study of Hebrews.

_____

_____

_____

9. What are some of the *"signs and wonders and various miracles and by gifts of the Holy Spirit"* (2:4) that God uses to validate the salvation He provides? (See Acts 5:12-16; 1 Corinthians 12:4-11.)

_____

_____

_____

_____

❖ Hebrews 2:5-8a—A Testimony About the World to Come

10. Read Genesis 1:26-28. Record the facts that support the view of man's worth and his dominion over all created things.

_____

_____

_____

_____

11. From Hebrews 2:6-8, list those phrases that refer to Jesus specifically and to mankind in general.

_____

_____

_____

12. From the verses you just looked at, what do you learn about your significance in God's eyes?

_____

_____

_____

❖ Hebrews 2:8b-9—"We See Jesus"

13. In Hebrews 1:4, Jesus is said to be *"superior to angels,"* while in Hebrews 2:9, that *"for a little while [He] was made lower than the angels."* How do you understand both statements to be true?

_____

_____

_____

Apply what you have learned. Just as Jesus, while on earth, did not display the full magnitude of His glory, His followers will receive more glory in the life to come: *"If [we are God's] children, then heirs—heirs of God and fellow heirs with Christ, provided we suffer with Him in order that we may also be glorified with Him. For I consider that the sufferings of this present time are not worth comparing with the glory that is to be revealed to us"* (Romans 8:17-19). We have a rewarding eternal existence to look forward to because He "tasted death" (Hebrews 2:9) for us.

The Superiority of Christ
Hebrews 1:1–2:9

Superior to Angels

Using seven quotations from the Old Testament, five from Psalms, the author argues that Christ is superior to angels. These show that God has never spoken to an angel in the way He addresses Christ. The first quotation, from Psalm 2:7, gives the term *"My Son"* with a significance that surpasses possible fulfillment by any mere human or angel. Jesus Christ is *Son* in a way that no other being is. No angel inherits the name *"Son"* (Hebrews 1:5). Because He is God, only the Son assumes a position of authority at the throne of God.

The second quotation echoes the Lord's promise to David and His words to Jesus at His baptism and the Transfiguration. Also included is the message of an angel to Mary announcing the impending birth of Jesus, *"He ... will be called the Son of the Most High"* (Luke 1:32).

The third quotation comes from the song of Moses (Deuteronomy 32), which was often used in temple services. Hebrews 1:6 speaks of Christ as one whom angels worship. *"Firstborn,"* a title for Jesus, means *prior* and *unique*. Jesus is the pre-existing, eternal Son. The song of Moses originally addressed worship to *Yahweh*. Having established Jesus' deity, the author includes the Son in worship that belongs to the Father.

The next quotation, from Psalm 104:4, can be interpreted to mean that wind and fire do God's bidding. Another view suggests that His angels, who are His servants, are as swift as the wind and as powerful as flames of fire. This view places angels above humans, but far below the place of the Son.

Next, quoting Psalm 45:6-7, the author stresses the Messiah's sovereign and eternal nature. Unlike earthly kings ruling kingdoms that rise only to fall, God's Anointed One is the ruler of a kingdom that has no end. Then the following thought is added: *"Uprightness is the scepter of Your kingdom"* (1:8). This is no ordinary kingdom, it is one ruled by righteousness: *"You have loved righteousness and hated wickedness"* (1:9). Because love governs over all, the subjects of such a kingdom need never fear the corruption of power and authority.

Because Christ is this king, God has anointed Him with the *"oil of gladness"* and placed Him above His companions. His anointing does not refer to any particular time, because Jesus Christ is the Anointed One from eternity to eternity. Probably *"Your companions"* refers to the *"many sons"* (2:10) whom the firstborn Son calls His *"brothers"* (2:11). They are also the saints, the followers of Jesus. He is the heir, and they are His joint heirs.

Think about how Psalm 45:6-7 links Christ's love for righteousness with His joy (*"gladness"*). Our joy comes from Him. He has promised that those who obey Him will remain in His love. As a result, His joy is in us and is complete (John 15:10-11). This is different from happiness that arises from circumstances. This joy is rooted in our unchanging Lord and His righteousness, while circumstances are subject to change. As our longing for Jesus and His righteousness increases, our sinful desires lessen and the result is joy!

In the sixth quote, the writer applies the reference to God from Psalm 102:25-27 to Christ. What is true of one is true of the other. Verse 10 reminds us that God's Son was active in Creation and pre-existed as God the Son. What was created can, like a garment, be changed or discarded, but God does not change; He remains forever. The present tense in verse 11 (*"You remain"*) contrasts the permanence of the Son with the passing nature of created things.

The final quotation, from Psalm 110:1, echoes the description of the Son being seated at God's right hand. Jesus applied those words to Himself at His trial. God will make the Messiah's enemies powerless. No angel sits in a place of victory and honor at God's right hand.

Angels serve not only God, but also *"those who are to inherit salvation"* (1:14). Salvation includes all we have already received in Christ as well as final deliverance when Christ returns. The angels *serve* Christ's saints, but only the Son can *save*. The same question begins and ends this series of quotes, bringing us full circle to the answer: God did not speak to any angel in the way He addresses His Son.

A Warning

"Therefore" connects the facts about Christ's greatness to a warning in chapter 2: We are responsible to pay attention to so great a message of salvation. The writer acknowledges that in every person is a tendency to wander. He warns Christians who have heard and accepted the gospel to hold fast to their faith. Like a boat drifting toward rapids, the Christians addressed here were at a danger point. They must resist an enemy ready to distract them from true faith. Jesus suffered and died to become *"the founder of ... salvation"* (2:10). The gift is precious and complete. If we neglect it, we shall not escape the consequence.

Think about how Hebrews warns against gradual drifting from the life of faith, not against deliberate sin. C. S. Lewis has pointed out that small sins can separate us from God just as well as big sins. Drifting away from God requires only one thing: passive disregard of our great salvation.

Christ's Humiliation and Exaltation

The writer uses Psalm 8:4-6 to show the honor God has given people in the plan of creation. He has made humans a little lower than the angels, yet has given mankind power and control over the earth (Genesis 1:26). But the Fall changed Adam's dominion over creation.

Christ, as the second Adam, fulfilled the psalm's prophetic message by being *"made ... lower than the angels"* (2:7). Christ humbled Himself when He came to earth as a man. This is called the Incarnation. Only in this way could He represent us before the Father. Grace required that Christ suffer and die. Yet, He who was humbled has been received into heaven, crowned with glory and honor. God decreed that—after His work as a servant—all would be subject to Him.

Personalize this lesson.

✓ To accomplish salvation, the Son of God became, for a little while, lower than the angels. He is now crowned with glory and honor because He suffered death for everyone. Revering angels, who are God's servants, dishonors the Son. He became a man, not an angel. He shares our humanity and elevates our value. We must reject any teaching that would place angels or any other created beings as mediators between God and us. *"For there is one God, and there is one Mediator between God and men, the Man Christ Jesus, who gave Himself as a ransom for all"* (1 Timothy 2:5). He alone is worthy of worship.

The Excellence of Christ
Hebrews 2:10–3:6

❖ Hebrews 2:10-12—For the Father's Purpose

1. Hebrews 2:9 quotes Psalm 8 and applies it to Jesus. Using a standard or Bible dictionary, define:

   a. *glory*_____

   _____

   b. *honor*_____

   _____

2. What do each of the following passages teach about glory?

   a. Isaiah 42:5-9 _____

   _____

   _____

   b. Romans 6:4 _____

   _____

   _____

3. How is Jesus *"the founder of ... salvation"* (Hebrews 2:10)?

   _____

   _____

4. Identify the two subjects mentioned in Hebrews 2:11.

   _____

   _____

❖ Hebrews 2:13-15—By the Son's Service

5. Read the following passages: Luke 4:5-13; John 8:42-45;
    1 Peter 5:8. From the Hebrews passage and the verses you read,
    write three or four words or phrases about the devil.

    _____

    _____

6. How do people today view the devil?

    _____

    _____

7. Why do you think people fear death?

    _____

    _____

8. What does it mean to you that Jesus frees us from the fear of
    death (2:15)?

    _____

    _____

    _____

❖ Hebrews 2:16-17—For the Believer's Sake, Part 1

9. According to Galatians 3:6-7, who are *"the sons of Abraham"*?

    _____

10. From Leviticus 16:3-5, 15-22, 34, give

    a. a brief description of the duties of the high priest

        _____

        _____

    b. the meaning of *propitiation*

        _____

        _____

11. Verse 17 describes Jesus as a merciful and faithful High Priest. *Merciful* means *compassionate, kind,* and *forgiving. Faithful* means *true to His promises, devoted,* and *loyal.* How do the words *merciful* and *faithful* influence your feelings about Jesus as High Priest?

_____

_____

_____

❖ Hebrews 2:18–3:1—For the Believer's Sake, Part 2

12. Read Mark 1:40-41 and Luke 19:1-10. What does each passage tell you about the help Jesus offers?

_____

_____

_____

13. What does Jesus promise, as recorded in Matthew 7:7-11 and 11:28-30?

_____

_____

14. Reread Hebrews 2:17–3:1. What comfort do you receive from the truth contained in these verses?

_____

_____

_____

❖ Hebrews 3:2-6—Greater Honor Belongs to the Son

15. What things about Moses made him great? (See Exodus 2:1-10; 3:1-10; Deuteronomy 34:10-12.)

_____

_____

_____

_____

16. In what ways is Jesus said to be even greater than Moses?

_____

_____

17. The author of Hebrews uses *"house"* seven times in these five verses. What do you think he means when he says we are God's "house"?

_____

_____

18. Use the following verses to develop your ideas of courage and hope. In your own words, write a few sentences explaining your ideas.

   a. *courage* (Deuteronomy 1:21; Acts 27:25)

   _____

   _____

   b. *hope* (Romans 15:13; 1 Thessalonians 1:3)

   _____

   _____

19. In what way should these Christian concepts of *courage* and *hope* affect your daily life?

_____

_____

_____

Apply what you have learned. How does the fact that Jesus *"is not ashamed to call* [us] *brothers"* (2:11) inspire you to love Him? Want to please Him? Want to bring Him glory? What is one thing you can do today to demonstrate your love for Him as your Brother?

The Excellence of Christ
Hebrews 2:10–3:6

Christ's humiliation and death suggest the seriousness of sin. To deal with the power of evil, God had to sacrifice His sinless Son. The value of Christ's triumph over death led the author to write about this great salvation.

Perfected Through Suffering

The Jews expected their Messiah to be a powerful king. The idea of a humble, suffering Savior offended them. Here, however, the writer tells why it was fitting that God chose a lowly path for His Son; salvation could be accomplished only in this way. The emphasis on the Lord's humility and suffering is a necessary part of the author's continuing argument for Christ's superiority. The process of salvation is that of *"bringing many sons to glory"* (Hebrews 2:10). In fulfilling His work of salvation, Christ's suffering and humility resulted in glory—His own and ours.

As our forerunner and representative, Jesus experienced physical birth and death. In His birth, the Son accepted humanity's weakness (Philippians 2:6-11). But, unlike the human experience, Christ demonstrated strength and superiority through His death. The Son has entered into God's presence, securing the entry of those He has redeemed. Verse 10 also describes Jesus as being made *"perfect through suffering,"* meaning to *fulfill a certain goal*. By suffering, Jesus completed perfectly the work the Father had given Him and removed the sins of those *"who are sanctified"* (Hebrews 2:11).

The result of His suffering is that believers not only are saved but also are *"sanctified"* (meaning *set apart for God's use*). Jesus set Himself apart to become our Savior, and by His sacrifice we are set apart from the corruption of sin to honor and serve God. The link between Jesus and those He saves and sanctifies is emphasized in the words *"are of the same family"* (Hebrews 2:11, NIV). Jesus is not ashamed to call us members of His family.

Three Old Testament passages demonstrate Jesus' identification with us. Using Psalm 22:22, the author confirms that Jesus calls His followers *"brothers."* From Isaiah 8:17 he shows that, although He was God, while on earth, Jesus depended on the Father in complete trust. Isaiah 8:18 shows that Jesus stands faithfully with His brothers, as the prophet Isaiah had been faithful to his children.

Unlike any other death, Jesus' death broke Satan's grip on humanity by making death a passage to glory for any who would join the family of faith. Jesus became the author of salvation by defeating the devil and the sting of death itself. His resurrection means that even death cannot separate Christ's people from the love of God; no longer is the threat of death a means of intimidation.

Hebrews 2:17 introduces one of the book's major themes: To save mankind, Jesus had to be like fallen man in every way, yet without sin. Jesus was therefore qualified to represent us before God as our great High Priest. Only Hebrews develops this aspect of the Savior's work. A priest represents people before God and represents God to the people. Israel's priesthood served as a *type*, pointing to the ultimate priesthood of Christ. At the close of His earthly life, Jesus offered Himself on the Cross to pay for sin; thus man was reconciled to God.

In verse 18, the writer underscores the reason Jesus is sufficient and able to represent us before God. He is merciful because His suffering and trials enable Him to sympathize with ours. He is faithful because He completed the Father's purpose for His life without faltering.

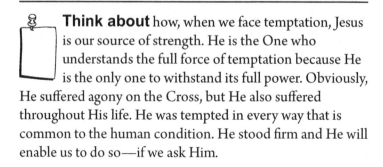

Think about how, when we face temptation, Jesus is our source of strength. He is the One who understands the full force of temptation because He is the only one to withstand its full power. Obviously, He suffered agony on the Cross, but He also suffered throughout His life. He was tempted in every way that is common to the human condition. He stood firm and He will enable us to do so—if we ask Him.

One Greater Than Moses

For the Jews, Moses occupied an unparalleled place before God. He led them out of Egypt and through the Red Sea, met God face-to-face, and received the tablets of the Law (Exodus 34:29-32). The author now shows that the Son is superior to the human lawgiver (Moses), and that Christ's New Covenant is superior in every way to the Old Covenant that has been replaced.

"Therefore" (3:1) introduces a conclusion to the argument begun in 2:11, where Jesus' identification with us paved the way to His being our High Priest. Jesus is referred to as *"the apostle and high priest of our confession."* An *apostle* is *one who is commissioned and sent*, and has the authority to speak on behalf of his sponsor. Thus the ministry of Moses, an apostle sent to speak on behalf of God, and Aaron, who as the high priest represented the people before God, are combined in one person, Jesus Christ, and He *"was faithful to Him who appointed Him."*

"House" (3:2) is used to symbolize the people of God. Moses' relationship to God's household was that of a servant and administrator in the house, whereas Christ's relationship to it is that of the Son and heir. Moses' role in the household was to serve, and he faithfully did so; Christ's role is to rule by the Father's appointment. The author does not minimize Moses' value; he wishes only to prove Christ's superiority.

Faith is God's gift to people and, as the Bible teaches, it is the believer's responsibility to continue living by it. Our author assures the readers that they, and he, are part of God's household if they all hold on to their courage and hope. Faithfulness is not a requirement laid only upon God and special servants such as Moses; it is the requirement of all His people. For this, we must focus our attention on Jesus.

Personalize this lesson.

✓ If difficult circumstances foster spiritual growth, and courage and hope are essential means for growth, then we understand why the author tells us to hold on! When the going is rough, courage moves us forward and hope trains our eye on the goal God has promised. Courage enables us to proceed on our course with firmness and without being paralyzed by fear. Courage is a gift from God: *"For God gave us not a spirit of fear but of power and love and self-control"* (2 Timothy 1:7). Hope, too, is a work of the Spirit (see Romans 15:13). Hope holds on to what God has promised. Do you need fresh courage or hope for the difficult circumstances you face? Ask Him for them! Believe that He will supply what you need so that you can hold on!

The Peril of Unbelief
Hebrews 3:7-19

❖ **Hebrews 3:7-11—Look to the Past and Learn About Consequences**

1. Why do you think the author used the words, *"as the Holy Spirit says,"* in verse 7?

   _____

   _____

2. In 10 words or less, what is the message of verses 7-11?

   _____

   _____

   _____

3. In Psalm 78:32-37, what characteristics are revealed about the Israelites during the Exodus period?

   _____

   _____

4. Who is the speaker in verse 10?

   _____

5. Explain to the best of your ability these phrases from verses 10-11:

   a. *"They always go astray in their heart."*

   _____

   _____

b.   *"They have not known My ways."*

_____

_____

_____

c.   *"They shall not enter My rest."*

_____

_____

_____

❖ Hebrews 3:12-14—Look to the Present and Prevent Sorrow

6.   Read 2 Peter 1:5-8 with Hebrews 3:12. From these passages, what can believers do to guard their hearts so they don't *"fall away from the living God"*?

_____

_____

_____

_____

7.   Read Ephesians 4:29-32 with Hebrews 3:13. From these verses, what can believers do to encourage and aid one another in the maturing of faith?

_____

_____

_____

_____

8.   What are the similarities between Hebrews 3:6 and 3:14?

_____

_____

_____

_____

❖ Hebrews 3:15-17—Let the Circumstances Be a Warning

9. Why do you think the author repeats the words of Psalm 95:7-8 in Hebrews 3:7-8 and 15?

10. Summarize the historical situation to which the author refers. (See Numbers 13:25-14:24.)

11. Read verses 16-17. To whom do these questions refer?

12. Reread Hebrews 2:2-4. To whom is the author of Hebrews asking the question in verse 3?

13. How do Hebrews 2:2-4 and 3:16-17 relate to you?

❖ Hebrews 3:18-19—"We See" the Reason for Loss

14. Why did God withdraw the benefit of rest from a generation of Israelites?

_____

_____

_____

15. How is unbelief fostered in our own time?

_____

_____

_____

16. What words and ideas come to mind when you think of *"His rest"* (3:18)?

_____

_____

_____

_____

17. Has there been an occasion in your life when a specific choice was pivotal in your spiritual or personal growth? How did your choice make a difference?

_____

_____

_____

_____

Apply what you have learned. We constantly face choices, and our decisions can have important consequences. In what way do you sometimes waver in doubt rather than trusting God? Will you choose to turn from unbelief, and instead, encourage faith in your own life and in the lives of others?

The Peril of Unbelief
Hebrews 3:7-19

A Warning From Scripture and History

The author of Hebrews wants to encourage his readers to persevere in their faith. He warns that if they make the same mistakes their countrymen made in the past, they will miss God's blessing. The Israelites are an example of how unbelief leads to disobedience, to falling away from the faith, and to the forfeit of God's blessing of rest.

"Therefore" connects verses 7-12 to the warning of verse 6—the readers should faithfully remain in God's household. The quote from Psalm 95:7-11 is introduced as a statement by the Holy Spirit. *"Today"* reminds readers that they live daily in an era of grace—a time in which the Son speaks for the Father, and that will last only until God's appointed time of judgment. The plea is strong: *"Do not harden your hearts"* (3:8). In Scripture the heart signifies the mind, emotions, and will. Refusal to listen produces hardness of heart. However, the *"do not"* indicates hope. Such a fate can be avoided.

The quotation from Psalm 95:7-11 deals with situations where the Israelites rebelled against God in the desert. One incident occurred when there was no water. Israel responded poorly to the crisis (Exodus 17:1-7). The narrative ends with *"he called the name of the place Massah* [testing] *and Meribah* [quarreling], *because of the quarreling of the people ... and because they tested the LORD."* The psalm uses *"Meribah"* and *"Massah,"* but in Hebrews 3:8, where the psalm is quoted, *"rebellion"* and *"testing"* are used. The second incidence of rebellion caused God to swear that the Israelites would not enter His rest. Twelve spies returned from investigating the Promised Land. Caleb and Joshua praised the land and Israel's ability under God to overcome their enemies. The people chose to believe the discouraging report of the other spies. Deliberate disbelief in God caused their hearts to harden.

"They always go astray in their heart; they have not known My ways" (3:10). The intellectual knowledge of what God requires is not denied here; what is denied is Israel's acceptance of God's leadership. The quotation from Psalm 95 continues, *"As I swore in My wrath"* (3:11).

God's anger is a response to continued disobedience. Man's disobedience was the cause; God's oath, the result. In the days of Moses, a generation of Israelites was kept out of the Promised Land because of their unbelief. Centuries later, the psalmist urged the people to enter into God's promised rest. Now, the author of Hebrews also urges his readers to walk in faith lest they, too, be kept out of that promised rest. *Rest* once meant only a place; now it also means an experience. God invites us to share with Him daily fellowship and peace, and then, finally, a place— heaven itself.

Consequences of Unbelief

The words *"take care"* suggest the author's concern over his readers' spiritual condition. He points out parallels between the Israelites' condition and that of the Hebrew Christians. With the aid of key words from the psalm, he shows that unbelief and turning away with a hardened heart must not be allowed.

In 3:12, the writer selects a future tense: *"Take care ... lest there be in any of you an evil, unbelieving heart."* He presents a future fact rather than possibility, signaling great urgency. He is emphatic yet hopeful. Relaxation of belief will lead to apostasy, but the choice to prevent that is presently before the people. From chapter to chapter, the urging to strong faith while it is still possible leaps off the page. The danger of *"fall*[ing] *away from the living God"* is more than a possibility, but not a fact—not yet. The danger stated, literally, is *to apostatize*, to *grow faithless*, *to deliberately rebel against God*—the final act of unbelief. To depart from Christ or lose hold on Him is to fall away from the living God. The words point to the power of God, who will not overlook rebellion.

In verse 13, the author urges Christians who are strong to help the weak and encourage one another daily. *"Today"* emphasizes that believers still have the chance to do what is right, for they live in the day of grace. The opportunity will end for all of them at Christ's return, or for each

of them at their own death. They are warned to be on guard against sin
and to avoid being tricked by Satan and subtly led, without resistance, to
unbelief.

Think about how the phrases *"an evil, unbelieving
heart"* (3:12) and *"the deceitfulness of sin"* (3:13) link
sin and unbelief. One produces the other, and they
feed on each other. We must heed the warning about
having an unbelieving heart or being hardened by sin's
deceitfulness. Our responsibility is also not just for
ourselves. We must encourage one another. Our actions, not
just our words, should inspire and encourage others: *"Let
each of us please his neighbor for his good, to build him up"*
(Romans 15:2). If we earnestly try to keep our own hearts
right before God and encourage others in their efforts to do
so, we can interrupt the vicious circle of an unbelieving heart
and the deceitfulness of sin.

By using a series of questions, the author analyzes rebellion, retribution,
and the reason for both. The second question in verse 16 actually
answers the first. Who rebelled? Those who saw and enjoyed God's
miraculous deliverance and provision. During the 40 years of desert
life, the Israelites' continued stubbornness and rebellion provoked the
Lord to anger. Punishment came as a holy vindication of God's moral
character and His authority over the people. The Israelites were kept
out of the Promised Land because of their disobedience brought on by
unbelief.

After a skillful presentation of Scripture, history, and logical argument,
the author concludes that Israel failed to enter the land because of
unbelief. The Israelites could not enter God's rest because they rejected
His requirements of love and obedience.

Personalize this lesson.

☑ This strong warning against sin and unbelief was not written to new Christians. In spite of spiritual growth, we never reach a place in our journey where turning from the path is no longer a danger. This letter was written to redirect Christians who had drifted from the truth or were tolerating sin.

It is important for us to continually maintain a close and trusting relationship with the Lord. If we neglect reading, studying, and obeying the Bible—if we decide we have already heard everything we need to know—we put ourselves at risk. Is there some aspect of your spiritual life that needs shoring up? What steps can you take today to make it right? Peter gave sound advice: *"Be sober-minded; be watchful. Your adversary the devil prowls around like a roaring lion, seeking someone to devour. Resist him, firm in your faith"* (1 Peter 5:8-9).

Lesson 5

God's Promised Rest
Hebrews 4:1-13

Memorize God's Word: Hebrews 4:12.

❖ Hebrews 4:1-2—The Past As a Warning

1. What does the author warn against in Hebrews 3:19–4:2?

    _____

    _____

    _____

2. Why is the author's warning still so important for Christians today (4:1)?

    _____

    _____

3. Why is it not enough to only *hear* the gospel?

    _____

    _____

❖ Hebrews 4:3-6—God's Past and Present Rest

4. According to John 5:15-21 and Ephesians 1:17-21, what sort of *work* is God continuing to do?

    _____

    _____

    _____

5. Read John 14:23-27. What aspects of God's rest do you find in this passage?

    _____

    _____

    _____

❖ Hebrews 4:7-9—The Meaning of *"Today"*

6. Review Hebrews 4:1-9. Locate and briefly describe the different *rests* in this passage.

    _____

    _____

    _____

    _____

7. What is the author suggesting when he says a *"Sabbath rest"* *"remains"* (4:9)?

    _____

    _____

    _____

8. Read Joshua 1:1-3; 13:1 and Judges 1:1; 2:6-13. What does Hebrews 4:8 confirm?

    _____

    _____

    _____

❖ Hebrews 4:10-11—The Work of Resting

9. According to John 6:28-35, what *work* must those who follow God do? (See also Galatians 3:1-3.)

    _____

    _____

    _____

10. How do you understand that we must *"strive to enter that rest"* (Hebrews 4:10-11)?

    _____

    _____

    _____

11. According to 2 Peter 1:4, what are two results of believing and obeying God's promises?

    _____

    _____

    _____

❖ Hebrews 4:12-13—Respecting the Word of God

12. What qualities of God's Word do you find in 4:12?

    _____

    _____

    _____

    _____

13. What does the Word of God do?

    _____

    _____

    _____

14. How could verse 13

    a. be a warning?_____

        _____

        _____

    b. offer comfort? _____

        _____

        _____

15. From 4:12-13, what do you learn about God that has an impact
    on you personally?

    _____

    _____

    _____

    _____

Apply what you have learned. In chapter 4,
God's universal, infinite knowledge is emphasized:
"*No creature is hidden from His sight, but all are naked
and exposed to the eyes of Him to whom we must give account*"
(4:13). How fearful and threatening this would be if God
were not perfectly loving and willing to forgive and forget
our sins. "*He who confesses* [his sins] *and forsakes them will
obtain mercy*" (Proverbs 28:13).

As believers, we can "bare our souls" to God and know
that He will not withdraw His love. It is impossible to
"hide" our sins from God; if we try to do that, we are
only deceiving ourselves. How open and honest is your
relationship with God?

Lesson 5 Commentary

God's Promised Rest
Hebrews 4:1-13

Hebrews 4 continues the warning, begun in chapter 3, to Christians whose trust in Christ was being eroded. The author wants to show that God's rest, in and through Christ, is still available to those who listen to God with pliable hearts. To be at rest is to be at peace with God, free from feelings of anxiety or defeat. Rest also includes the idea of being established in Christ—remaining confident in His salvation.

Rest for God's People

The author urges his readers to be watchful so that no one falls short of the rest God offers. *"Fail to reach"* pictures a racer failing to finish the course. After sounding the warning, the author points to the *course* (faith) on which the Christian must stay. Faith is the essential requirement for salvation and its benefits.

The Israelites in the desert heard God's good news of rest, but the message did not benefit them because they failed to have faith. God swore that because of their unbelief the Israelites would not enter into His rest—yet His rest stands ready for any who, by faith, will enter it.

The last part of verse 3 shifts to the topic of *work*. God entered into His rest when He finished His work at Creation.

Rest does not imply that God was weary from His work of creation, but that He ceased from it. Neither does it imply that God has not been active since that time or that He does not govern the world He made.

Verses 4-5 support verse 3 by citing two Old Testament sources. The first—*"For He has somewhere spoken about the seventh day"* (4:4)—is an indirect reference to Genesis 2:2. God's *"rest"* must not be understood as a limited time of rest. Unlike the six days used for Creation, the seventh day has no night to close it, and it continues to the present. The establishment of the Sabbath day, with its call to set aside work, reminds us of God's rest.

Think about how you keep the Sabbath. Jesus said *"The Sabbath was made for man, not man for the Sabbath"* (Mark 2:27). That day was—and is— beneficial to people's physical nature and essential to our spiritual nature. How could you gain more spiritual, emotional, and physical benefit from Sabbath rest?

The author of Hebrews intends to convince his readers that the divine warnings and promises apply to them just as they did to the Israelites in the days of Moses or David. If they treat the saving message lightly, they will forfeit His rest. He appeals again, *"Do not harden your hearts"* (4:7).

The statement *"if Joshua had given them rest"* (4:8) implies in a new way that God's rest remains available today. The words for *Joshua* and *Jesus* are the same in the Greek Bible. The original language sets forth an argument by comparison between the *Jesus (Joshua)* who led his followers into partial rest in the earthly Canaan and the *Jesus (the Son of God)* who leads the heirs of the New Covenant into their complete and eternal rest.

God spoke of *"another day,"* which suggests that an unrealized rest remains for God's people. Verse 6 states that some will enter into this rest. The word used so far for *rest* referred to the land God promised Israel. Now *"Sabbath rest"* is introduced; it comes from a verb meaning *I keep the Sabbath.* God's rest after Creation began an experience that His people would join in continually keeping: an eternal rest. *"The people of God"* (4:9) indicates the true spiritual character of all believers. Scripture insists that faith qualifies God's people. Heaven is a future home and holy rest; foretastes of it come in this life. Hebrews 4:10 anticipates the full reality of Sabbath-rest—the final day when we cease from all striving and enter life in its fullest experience in the presence of Jesus Christ.

Exhortation to Enter God's Rest

Verse 11 urges watchfulness and diligence. It may sound contradictory
strive to enter rest, for God's grace alone brings us into His rest; but it
does so by His Word, which we must hear, receive, and obey through
faith. Anyone who falls will be guilty of the same kind of disobedience
the Israelites gave in to long ago.

Think about how the Sabbath rest is both present
and future—partial in this life, but fully realized only
in the life to come. Because we are "in process," we
must not be lethargic. We are to persevere until our
rest is complete, focusing on obedience to God. Yet we are not
to be anxious. Our present goal is inner serenity. Jesus said,
*"Come to Me, all who labor and are heavy laden, and I will give
you rest. Take My yoke upon you, and learn from Me, for I am
gentle and lowly in heart, and you will find rest for your souls. For
My yoke is easy, and My burden is light"* (Matthew 11:28-30).

Unlike man's word, God's word is eternally alive and effective, bringing
blessing to those who receive and obey it and pronouncing judgment on
those who disregard it. Four things are claimed concerning it. It is *"living
... active, sharper than any two-edged sword,"* and it *pierces* (Hebrews 4:12).
The Greek meaning for *active* means *full of energy* and suggests that God's
word has an effective, dynamic capability to bring about His purposes.

The word of God cuts through the innermost parts of a person to judge
"the thoughts and intentions of the heart." Not only does God expose guilt
and fault, He uncovers motives; He reaches developing goodness and
embryonic faith; He understands and rightly judges life experiences that
shape the behavior of each individual. God's word eliminates confusion
and distortion, which is good news!

It may be possible to hide the inner being from other people, and
at times even from ourselves, but nothing escapes God's careful
examination. The word of God reveals the emotional and spiritual aspect
of a person more surely than the latest scientific and medical processes
reveal the physical. It can confront and wound; it can comfort and heal.

Personalize this lesson.

☑ The passage concludes with the reminder that the Word of God judges us. That would be a fearful thing, except that our God, the Holy One, knows us through and through and still loves us. He sees us not only as we are now, but as we will be when His good work in us is complete: *"Beloved, we are God's children now, and what we will be has not yet appeared; but we know that when He appears we shall be like Him, because we shall see Him as He is"* (1 John 3:2). Will you talk to God about the feelings this lesson has stirred in you?

Lesson 6

A Great High Priest
Hebrews 4:14-5:10

Memorize God's Word: Hebrews 4:15-16.

❖ Hebrews 4:14-16—The Distinction of Jesus

1. What are the distinctive characteristics of Jesus' priesthood shown in verse 14?

   _____

   _____

2. How does knowing what kind of priest Jesus is help us *"hold fast our confession"*?

   _____

   _____

3. State in your own words the truths found in verses 15-16.

   _____

   _____

   _____

❖ Hebrews 5:1-3—The Identification of a Priest

4. Leviticus 9:1-7 records the beginning of the priests' ministry in Israel. Cite the verses you use to answer the following questions.
   a. Who is the designer of the sacrificial system?

   _____

b.   What are the purposes of the offerings?

_____

_____

5.   Read Leviticus 16:1-6, 11, 15-17 with Hebrews 5:1-3. State at least three facts about the work or person of a high priest.

_____

_____

_____

_____

❖ Hebrews 5:4-6—The Selection of Jesus

6.   How is a high priest chosen?

_____

_____

7.   Exodus 28–29 describes the great honor and respect given to the position of priest. Why does that make it seem even more remarkable that *"Christ did not exalt Himself to be made a high priest, but was appointed"* (5:5)?

_____

_____

8.   The quotes in verses 5 and 6 come from Psalms 2 and 110. Read these two psalms, then list additional things you learn about the Messiah.

_____

_____

_____

_____

9.   Read Genesis 14:18-20; Hebrews 7:1-4. Who is Melchizedek?

_____

_____

❖ Hebrews 5:7-8—The Qualifications of Jesus

10. What did Jesus do during His life on earth that was like the ministry of the high priest?

_____

_____

_____

11. When was verse 7 fulfilled in Jesus' life as recorded in the Gospels (Luke 22:41-44)?

_____

_____

_____

❖ Hebrews 5:9-10—The Designation of Jesus

12. The words *perfect* and *mature,* which often have the same meaning in Scripture, can be defined as *complete beyond improvement, fully developed.* Explain how *perfect* or *mature* is used in each of the following verses:

    a. Ephesians 4:13 _____

    _____

    _____

    b. Hebrews 6:1_____

    _____

    _____

    c. James 1:4_____

    _____

    _____

13. Read John 3:1-8, 16-17; 1 Peter 1:18-21. Explain how Jesus *"became the source of eternal salvation"* (Hebrews 5:9).

_____

_____

14. How does your belief in Jesus as *"the source of eternal salvation"* affect your relationships with people who do not yet know Him as their Savior?

_____

_____

_____

_____

Apply what you have learned. Jesus has been *"appointed to act on behalf of* [us] *in relation to God"* (5:1). Is there any aspect of life that does not matter to God? Our physical and our spiritual needs are important to Him. *"Look at the birds of the air: they neither sow nor reap nor gather into barns, and yet your heavenly Father feeds them. Are you not of more value than they?"* (Matthew 6:26, 33). Everything that matters to us matters to Him! And because He understands and cares, we are encouraged to boldly approach Him to ask for help.

Lesson 6 Commentary

A Great High Priest
Hebrews 4:14-5:10

The Old Testament presents the Messiah as King and Priest, but in the New Testament, only the book of Hebrews develops the priestly doctrine of God's Son serving His people at the Father's throne.

We Approach God Through Christ

The author now enlarges on the theme of Jesus as the High Priest. *"Great"* describes Christ's priestly office to assert His superiority as the High Priest over all the high priests of Israel, including Aaron.

Once a year the high priest entered the Most Holy Place to offer sacrifices for his own sin and the sins of the people. Our great High Priest has proceeded through the heavens into God's presence. He has done in reality what the earthly high priest did symbolically. Using Jesus, His human name, binds Him to us and reminds us of His earthly life, His suffering, and His death. The phrase *"the Son of God"* also expresses His deity. The writer repeats the warning to hold tightly to faith.

In 4:15, the strongest reason for holding fast is stated: *"We do not have a high priest who is unable to sympathize with our weaknesses."* On the contrary, He sympathizes with the limitations of mankind. When He *"passed through the heavens"* (4:14), transcending all that is native to humankind, He did not discard His sympathetic heart. Now God has identified with humanity in a more individual, intimate way. He is the believers' High Priest and Mediator who sympathizes with their weaknesses. He knows how to help them because He shared their experiences, with one exception—He is without sin.

Jesus' resistance to the temptations to sin required strength of will and dependence on His Father. Like us, He faced the power of evil. Being tempted and yet sinless, He became a high priest who both understands and is qualified to help. His overcoming was far beyond any experience of endurance we might have and gives us hope.

Because of our High Priest, believers can *"approach the throne of grace with confidence"* (4:16, NIV). The throne of grace is where Jesus *"sits"* exalted at the Father's right hand. In earlier days, people drew near to God only through a high priest who served here on earth. Now, God may be approached through the heavenly High Priest, Jesus Christ. The word *throne* is appropriate to the idea of *grace,* for there the King-Priest dispenses His unmerited favor on those who deserve judgment.

Verse 14:16 states, *"that we may receive mercy and find grace."* Mercy is God's compassion on the guilty; *grace* is God's unearned provision for the helpless. It is implied that the believer's approach will be made in contrition and faith.

Think about how Jesus is our only source of help because He resisted the strongest pressures Satan could bring to bear against Him (2:18). The only way we will overcome is by His help, and to receive it, we must admit we need it. God wants us to come to Him for strength to withstand every temptation, whether "large" or "small," for in God's eyes there are no "small sins": *"One who is faithful in a very little is also faithful in much, and one who is dishonest in a very little is also dishonest in much"* (Luke 16:10). Because sin comes so naturally and easily for us, we need help each and every day.

Qualifications of a High Priest

The writer approaches Jesus' qualifications to serve as our high priest by pointing to what is true of *"every high priest"* (5:1). Three qualifications are necessary for the office: the high priest must share the same nature as those he represents before God; he must be appointed by God; he must be compassionate toward sinners. The priest's responsibility was to represent the people before God. In His humanity, Jesus was qualified to do this.

God alone could appoint a high priest to the task. Influenced by the beauty of the priestly garments and the awe surrounding the priest's duties, ambitious men could have sought the position, but God appointed a representative whose honor would be found in the humility of service. He performed a holy task for God and the people.

Christ's Qualifications as High Priest

Again, Psalm 2:7 is used to praise the Lord's superiority. In Hebrews 5:5 the quote shows that Jesus' work as our representative is the service of the Son of God, not mere man. Jesus and His work are far superior to the splendor of the Aaronic priesthood. The quotation in verse 6, from Psalm 110:4, applies specifically to the priesthood. *"The order of Melchizedek"* does not mean a *series of priests* stemming from Melchizedek but rather the *kind*. Melchizedek was unique; no father, mother, or sons are mentioned in Scripture. He was not of Aaron's line. He did not inherit his priesthood, nor did he transfer it to others. In these ways, Christ's priesthood was like Melchizedek's rather than like Aaron's.

Using Psalms 2 and 110, Jesus the Messiah is proven to be both King and Priest. His appointment as priest rises out of the eternal and superior order of Melchizedek. In Hebrews 5:7, the phrase *"Jesus offered up prayers and supplications"* uses language that refers to the priest offering sacrifices for the people, and provides evidence that Jesus acted as a priest long before He ascended into heaven.

In the Garden of Gethsemane, Jesus struggled to submit to death and separation from God as a substitute for sinful humanity. He walked the path of obedience and, by the sufferings that came His way, learned just what obedience involves under the conditions of human life on earth. He suffered, learned, and was *"made perfect,"* thus revealing the Father's "full" character. The word *perfect* gives the idea of *complete*. In other words, God's saving purposes have been perfectly fulfilled, or completed, through the suffering of Jesus Christ.

Christ satisfies the conditions of the high priesthood, and His priesthood goes far beyond that of the Levitical system. He did not enter a temple or tabernacle; He entered into the presence of God Himself, where He represents us at the throne of grace. For Christ to be only a prophet and king was not enough, for prophets proclaim and kings rule, but a priest brings the sacrifice for the forgiveness of sin. When Jesus was on the Cross and said, *"It is finished,"* He completed the offering and became the sacrifice, *"the source of eternal salvation to all who obey Him"* (5:9).

Personalize this lesson.

✓ This week's study emphasized that Christ, our High Priest, represents us before His Father by identifying with us in temptation and suffering. God's holy Son sympathizes with our weaknesses! Are you tempted? Suffering? Feeling weak? How does knowing that Jesus understands and sympathizes with you help? Remember that you can *"with confidence draw near to the throne of grace,* [and] *receive mercy and find grace to help in time of need"* (4:16). Take time this week to pour out your heart to Jesus. Ask for His mercy. Then rest silently in His presence for a few minutes, knowing that He is meeting you with grace.

The Perils of Apathy and Apostasy
Hebrews 5:11-6:8

❖ Hebrews 5:11-14—The Basic Position: Infancy

1. It is normal and healthy for babies to mature physically, emotionally, and mentally. When children fail to grow and mature, what is the impact on them? On those who care for them?

_____

_____

_____

2. What signs of delayed or arrested development does the author of Hebrews mention concerning the recipients of his letter?

_____

_____

3. What impact do you suppose this immaturity may have had on both the people themselves and the community they were part of?

_____

_____

_____

4. What do you think *"milk"* and *"solid food"* refer to in this passage?

_____

_____

_____

❖ Hebrews 5:14–6:3—The Basic Prompting: Leave/Go

5. According to verse 14, what do those who are *"mature"* do to grow spiritually?

   _____

   _____

6. In what practical area of your life do you need to learn to distinguish between good and evil?

   _____

   _____

7. What are some deeper concepts of spiritual maturity that you would like to explore?

   _____

   _____

   _____

8. *"Basic principles"* consist of information familiar to Jewish Christians. List the principles the author considers basic (6:1-2).

   _____

   _____

   _____

   _____

   _____

❖ Hebrews 6:4-6—The Basic Problem: Repentance

9. List the four elements of Christian experience cited in verses 4-5.

   _____

   _____

   _____

   _____

   _____

10. In your own words, what do you think the author hopes to accomplish by issuing this warning?

_____

_____

_____

_____

❖ Hebrews 6:7-8—The Basic Point: Purpose

11. What word picture does the author use in these verses, and what does it illustrate?

_____

_____

_____

_____

12. What happens to the land that produces a good crop?

_____

_____

_____

_____

13. What happens to the land that produces a bad crop?

_____

_____

_____

_____

14. What type of land best illustrates your Christian growth?

_____

_____

_____

_____

Apply what you have learned. *Walk, Don't Walk, Yield,* and *Caution* are familiar warnings on highway signs. They don't predict injury; in fact, they warn with the hope of preventing it. The passage we have just studied is similar to these warning signs. If people choose beliefs and behaviors that contradict the gospel, they put themselves in great danger. What should we do? We can pursue maturity, pay attention to warnings against indifference, guard against abandoning our faith, and train ourselves to *"distinguish good from evil"* by the *"constant practice"* of the *"solid food"* (5:14) of God's Word.

The Perils of Apathy and Apostasy
Hebrews 5:11–6:8

Because his readers are too immature to understand the significance of the Melchizedek priesthood, the writer of Hebrews exhorts them toward spiritual maturity before continuing his letter. To understand the message of Hebrews—the superiority of the New Covenant over the Old, of Christ over the sacrificial system—requires mature faith.

Failure to Progress in the Faith

Moral and spiritual laziness seem to prevent the original readers from understanding and applying truth. Though the Hebrews should have been instructing others, by now, they still needed elementary teaching.

"The basic principles of the oracles of God" (Hebrews 5:12) are the rudimentary teachings of God's Word. Spiritual immaturity inhibits understanding advanced Christian teaching. The writer uses the metaphors of milk and solid food to make his point. Milk is appropriate food for infants. After infancy, proper development demands solid food also.

"The word of righteousness" (5:13) includes teaching on the priestly function of Christ. It may also refer to the matter of what is right and wrong. The writer feels, though, a more thorough explanation of the relationship between Christ and Melchizedek depends on whether the readers are prepared to consider deeper truths. The mature believer partakes of deeper truths, acts on them, and *"by constant practice"* (5:14) develops knowledge based on experience of what is right and wrong.

Exhortation to Progress

"Therefore" (6:1), both teacher and reader are to to *"leave the elementary doctrine of Christ,"* not in the sense of throwing it aside, but in the sense

of growing past it to greater stature. *"Let us ... go on to maturity"* uses the word *mature* in the sense of *complete*.

🐝 **Think about** how Christian growth requires discipline, concentration. We don't automatically become mature. Spiritual growth requires effort. Paul's comparison of our spiritual development to an athlete's rigorous training applies as well to the study and application of God's Word: *"Every athlete exercises self-control in all things. They do it to receive a perishable wreath, but we an imperishable"* (1 Corinthians 9:25).

The writer stresses that the basics do not make up all Christian truth. He includes three groups of paired subjects that comprise the essentials of Christian teaching: (1) repentance and faith; (2) baptism and *"the laying on of hands,"* and (3) resurrection of the dead and judgment.

Hebrews 6:4-6 contain a solemn warning against *apostasy*—a *deliberate abandonment of the truth* so severe that the apostate person actually shames Christ. Such an extreme denial of God has no remedy because the only One who could bring them back has been rejected. The danger is not that of *falling into sin*, but of *willful opposition to God*. *"Those who have once been enlightened"* (6:4) seems to refer to people who have understood who Jesus is but have not moved beyond intellectual understanding to personal faith.

"Who have tasted the heavenly gift" may refer to eternal life, salvation, or Jesus. Some scholars interpret *tasting* to mean *eating*, but it can also imply *sampling*. The Greek word for *"shared"* in the next phrase—*"who ... have shared in the Holy Spirit"*—can refer to anyone who has been present when the Holy Spirit manifested Himself. Not everyone who witnesses manifestations of the Holy Spirit becomes personally filled with the Spirit. Verse 5, *"who ... have tasted the goodness of the word of God and the powers of the age to come,"* seems to imply, as did verse 4, tasting but not digesting the Word. Many heard the gospel and saw awesome miracles without moving on to personal faith.

"It is impossible, in the case of those who ... have fallen away, to restore them again to repentance" (6:4, 6) does not mean true believers' salvation

is lost. The apostates have hardened their hearts to the extent that repentance is not possible. They have totally rejected the Holy Spirit's work. The underlying reason is that *"they are crucifying once again the Son of God ... and holding Him up to contempt"* (6:6). The enormity of the sin is that they are repeating the same heinous act committed by the religious men who crucified Jesus because He said He was the Son of God. In their hearts they commit the same dreadful act.

Commentators are split on whether the people described in Hebrews 6:4-6 know God or merely know *about* God. If they really know God, can true believers lose their salvation? Consider the following points:

- ❖ If God is sovereign and His Word says His sheep will never perish, can we not rest in that assurance? (See John 10:28-29; Romans 8:29-39.)
- ❖ Our salvation depends solely on Christ's sacrificial death on the Cross for our sins. (See Galatians 2:15-16; Ephesians 2:8-9.).
- ❖ Paul speaks of the Holy Spirit being a seal, a guarantee of our salvation. Only God knows our hearts and exactly when we are sealed for eternity, but the Holy Spirit is the evidence (guarantee) that this has taken place and will be true forever. (See Romans 8:16; 2 Corinthians 1:21-22; Ephesians 1:11-14.)
- ❖ Though Hebrews 6:4-6 and 2 Peter 2:20-21 may seem to indicate that salvation can be lost, we must look at the Scriptures as a whole and see what truths are expressed throughout. Most scriptural evidence supports the conclusion that salvation is through grace alone, and that same grace ensures eternal life. Those who have hardened their hearts to the extent that the Holy Spirit can no longer work, and see no value in Jesus Christ and His death on the Cross, are the ones who need to worry.

The writer follows his warning with an illustration from nature. A field will yield whatever seed is buried in it, just like the human heart. God gives the blessing, but the heart must be free of *"thorns and thistles"* (6:8). To avoid reaping condemnation, everyone must carefully cultivate his or her own faith. The possibility of failure calls forth the warning, but the author reassures that *"in your case, beloved, we feel sure of better things"* (6:9).

Personalize this lesson.

Is this passage meant to "comfort the afflicted or afflict the comfortable?" The answer is most likely, "Yes." The one thing we must not do is doubt the mercy and grace of God. God never turns away a repentant sinner. However, we must be careful not to tolerate in ourselves an attitude of carelessness toward God's revealed truth. Is the Holy Spirit speaking comfort or conviction to you today? How will you respond to Him?

Lesson 8

The Certainty of God's Promises
Hebrews 6:9-20

❖ **Hebrews 6:9-10—Encourage**

1. Examine, phrase by phrase, the meaning of verse 9.

   a. *"Though we speak in this way"*— How had the author spoken?

   _____

   _____

   b. *"We feel sure"*— Why do you think the author is confident?

   _____

   _____

   c. *"Things that belong to salvation"*— What are some of these?

   _____

   _____

   _____

2. Read Matthew 25:40 and 1 Thessalonians 1:3 along with Hebrews 6:10. What motivates Christians to do good works?

   _____

   _____

   _____

   _____

   _____

❖ Hebrews 6:11-12—Implore

3. Read Colossians 1:10-12. What points from this passage complement the message of Hebrews 6:10-12?

_____

_____

_____

_____

4. Is the Holy Spirit pointing out anything to you concerning sluggishness in your relationship with God? Will you ask Him to help you with whatever He is showing you?

_____

_____

5. Why are *"faith and patience"* required to *"inherit the promises"*?

_____

_____

_____

❖ Hebrews 6:13-15—Explain

6. These verses contain a new train of thought. What in the preceding verses leads to the author's new discussion?

_____

_____

_____

_____

7. From what you know about Abraham's life, in what areas did he need patience?

_____

_____

_____

8. What is the longest that you have had to wait for God to fulfill an earnest request of yours?

_____

_____

_____

❖ Hebrews 6:16-18—Emphasize

9. From these three verses, record God's reasons for giving an oath along with His promise.

_____

_____

_____

_____

10. This message is addressed to *"we who have fled for refuge."* What do you think this means?

_____

_____

_____

_____

11. What contemporary occasions might require a person to flee for refuge and *"hold fast to ... hope"*?

_____

_____

_____

12. How does the Christian's concept of *hope* differ from the world's?

_____

_____

_____

_____

❖ Hebrews 6:19-20—Encourage

13. What does it mean to you to be *"sure and steadfast"* in hope?

_____

_____

_____

14. Explain the importance of an anchor to a boat.

_____

_____

_____

15. How has Jesus been your anchor in the storms of life?

_____

_____

_____

_____

_____

Apply what you have learned. Encouraging words fill these few verses. The author teaches that the Father initiates our safety, and the Lord Jesus guards it for us. We haven't earned God's kindness and care, yet God chooses to encourage us. You and I need to imitate Him by encouraging the people with whom we live and work and worship. Encouragement is often most needed when it is least deserved. Perhaps someone you know or love needs encouraging words from you right now.

The Certainty of God's Promises
Hebrews 6:9-20

After issuing the severe warnings of Hebrews 6:4-8, the writer states that he believes *"better things"* concerning his readers. Only here in this epistle is the Greek word *agapetos*—translated *"beloved,"* or *"dear friends"*(NIV)—used. The tenderness of the term offers reassurance.

True Believers Encouraged

"Better things ... that belong to salvation" (6:9) suggests a fruitful, spiritual life in contrast to a life that *"bears thorns and thistles."* The author's confidence rests on the foundation of God's righteousness and the past and present deeds of faith performed by the readers. God cannot *"overlook"* what they have done out of love for Him. Such love springs from true faith and expresses itself through practical love and deeds of kindness, which God considers as done for Him.

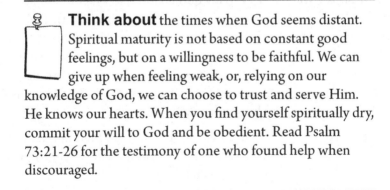

Think about the times when God seems distant. Spiritual maturity is not based on constant good feelings, but on a willingness to be faithful. We can give up when feeling weak, or, relying on our knowledge of God, we can choose to trust and serve Him. He knows our hearts. When you find yourself spiritually dry, commit your will to God and be obedient. Read Psalm 73:21-26 for the testimony of one who found help when discouraged.

In Hebrews 6:10-12, the author establishes three principles on which the Christian life is founded: *love, hope,* and *faith.* Christians are to *"love one another earnestly*" (1 Peter 1:22). They are to pursue the knowledge of God to establish their hope in Him. Hope is the answer to spiritual laziness; it will energize, encourage, excite, and motivate. Christian hope is sure, for it is grounded in God.

God has provided His Son and all Jesus Christ has done as a basis for the believer's hope. Now it is the believer's responsibility to hold to that knowledge until the end. This hope refers to assurance of salvation and includes a steadfast confidence in God's promises, including the coming glory promised by Christ. The author now examines other principles needed to secure this hope.

The readers of Hebrews are warned to *"not be sluggish"* (6:12). Those who endure and receive what is promised possess two qualities: *faith* and *patience*. Faith is confidence in God. Faith believes God, while hope energizes endurance. When applied to people, patience, or *longsuffering*, describes the willingness needed to endure when the promise is a long time coming to fulfillment. The Hebrew Christians are encouraged to imitate people who are examples of faith and patience. The reference in verse 12 applies to people of all ages, living or dead, who, by faith and patience, are sure of their coming inheritance, and even possess it by faith before life's close.

Using Abraham as an example of those who inherit the promises, verse 13 refers to the time when Abraham was willing to offer his promised son, Isaac, as a sacrifice to God. Because of his faith, Abraham received a great promise from God, partially quoted in verse 14. God not only promised Abraham numerous descendants, but also added that all nations would be blessed because of his obedience. Hope in that promise of Messianic salvation required the patience of centuries; it had to wait and not waver. That faith was rewarded, and the promised Messiah did come. Emphasis on the trustworthiness of God's promises is designed to strengthen hope when faith is faltering.

Genesis 22:16 is the first mention in Scripture of God binding Himself by an oath to keep His word. God could not, as men do, swear by one who is greater, for there is none greater than God.

God's Pledge

God's oath leaves no room for doubt regarding His purpose. *"The heirs of the promise"* are followers of God who walk by faith, including all those who received the promise—patriarchs, pre-Christian Jews, and Christians. God encourages faith by giving assurance so strong that even the weak in faith have reason for confidence. God, in taking an oath, did something similar to His taking on the limitations of human flesh. In taking an oath, He accommodates humanity's doubt instead of insisting that His character be trusted without any other assistance.

God's people now have two unchangeable possessions: God's promise and God's oath. Deception and lying are divine impossibilities because God is truth. How beautifully the author expresses God's kindness when he explains why God bothered with such detail: *"so that … we … might have strong encouragement"* (6:18).

"We who have fled for refuge" evokes the memory of Old Testament cities of refuge where those who accidentally killed someone could flee for safety. In the book of Psalms, God is described as *a refuge, a tower,* and *a hiding place.* As Christians, we are ever exposed to the world's corruption and the devil's frontal assaults and therefore need to *"hold fast to the hope set before us."* Jesus Christ is the basis of that hope. All hope of salvation and eternal life is based on the efficacy of Christ's work.

Our Hope

These Hebrew believers have been warned of possibly *"drifting"* (2:1), and nothing serves better to halt that tendency than an anchor. An anchor grips the ocean floor and holds a ship fast. From the strong, immovable anchor the author moves to another image. Hope penetrates *"the inner place behind the curtain"* (6:19). The writer is referring of the Most Holy Place in heaven into which Jesus has entered before us, implying that believers will follow Him there. He went *"to prepare a place for* [us]*"* (John 14:2).

The emphasis of this passage is on our hope and its source—the absolute reliability of God. An anchored ship may be buffeted back and forth but is never abandoned to the wind and the waves. The anchor limits what the storm can do. Like a ship, we will encounter storms, but we are never completely at their mercy. That is what Jesus meant when He said, *"In the world you will have tribulation. But take heart; I have overcome the world"* (John 16:33).

Personalize this lesson.

The storms of life are unavoidable realities through which faith and hope can develop. During "rough weather," we can be drawn closer to God, the source of our hope. How is life tossing you around right now? What specific promises of God offer you hope in your storm? Take some time to talk with God about the difficult circumstances you are in. Share both your thoughts and your feelings— then ask Him to increase your faith and hope so that when you come through this ordeal, you are even stronger.

Lesson 9

A Priest in the Order of Melchizedek
Hebrews 7

Memorize God's Word: Hebrews 7:24-25.

❖ **Hebrews 7:1-4—This Melchizedek**

1. Carefully read these verses along with the Genesis 14:18-20. List the ways in which Melchizedek is *"resembling the Son of God"* (7:3).

_____

_____

_____

_____

2. How do the following verses reveal Melchizedek's superiority to Abraham?
   a. Genesis 14:18-19

   _____

   _____

   b. Genesis 14:20b

   _____

   _____

❖ **Hebrews 7:5-10—Greater Than Abraham**

3. Who is Levi (Genesis 35:22-23; see also Numbers 3:1, 5-13)?

_____

4. What is the Law? (See Leviticus 18:1-5.)

    _____

    _____

    _____

5. What is a tithe? (See Leviticus 27:30-33.)

    _____

    _____

6. To someone who has lived under the Law, it might seem strange
    that Abraham paid a tithe to Melchizedek. Why might this have
    seemed strange? (See Numbers 18:21-24.)

    _____

    _____

7. Read Psalm 110:4. What does King David say about the Messiah
    in this verse?

    _____

    _____

8. *"It is beyond dispute"* (Hebrews 7:7) reveals certainty. What is the
    author convinced of as certain?

    _____

    _____

❖ Hebrews 7:11-17—The Power of One Greater

9. What does the author imply about the Aaronic priesthood in
    verse 11?

    _____

    _____

10. According to Hebrews 10:11-14; and 12:2, how does our author
    believe perfection occurs?

    _____

    _____

11. Verse 12 says that a *"change in the priesthood"* requires *"a change in the law."* How do the following verses express the characteristics of the "new" law?

    a. Romans 8:1-4

    _____

    _____

    b. Romans 13:8-10

    _____

    _____

12. How does the basis for Jesus' priesthood differ from that of the Levites? (See Hebrews 7:16.)

    _____

    _____

13. From Colossians 2:9-10, what is Jesus' superior qualification?

    _____

    _____

❖ Hebrews 7:18-25—Something Better Is Guaranteed

14. Why must the Law be *"set aside"* (7:18-19)?

    _____

    _____

15. Who swears the oath in verse 20?

    _____

    _____

16. List the phrases in verses 24-25 that make clear the *"better covenant"* (verse 22).

    _____

    _____

    _____

❖ Hebrews 7:26-28—The Proof of a Perfect Priest

17. What did Jesus offer up as a sacrifice for sin?

_____

_____

_____

18. How is Jesus, our High Priest, described in verse 26?

_____

_____

19. How does this description of the Son strengthen your
    confidence in Him as your High Priest?

_____

_____

_____

_____

Apply what you have learned. Anyone can
now approach God through the unique and perfect
high priest, Christ Jesus, who *"always lives to make
intercession for* [us]*"* (Hebrews 7:25). The sacrifices and
priestly service of the Old Covenant have ended forever.
They foreshadowed—and fulfilled in a limited and imperfect
way—this role that Christ now fills, that of being both the
priest and the sacrifice. Let your gratitude for *"such a great
salvation"* (2:3) overflow from your heart into your daily life
by offering "sacrifices" of praise and service.

A Priest in the Order of Melchizedek
Hebrews 7

The author uses the priest-king Melchizedek to explain Christ's superiority over the priesthood of the Mosaic Law. Jesus' superiority and permanence as our High Priest is the theme of Hebrews 7.

The Priority of the Melchizedek Priesthood

Melchizedek is mentioned twice in the Old Testament. Unlike any other Old Testament person, Melchizedek was both priest and king. His outstanding characteristics were righteousness (Hebrew *Melchi* means *my king*; *zedek* means *righteousness*) and peace (*Salem* means *peace*). He is similar to Christ by: (1) his titles *"king of righteousness"* and *"king of peace,"* (2) the absence of a family line descended from priests, and (3) his unstated origin and destiny.

Verses 1-10 present the superiority of the Melchizedek priesthood. (1) Melchizedek blessed Abraham, an event described as the greater person blessing the lesser. (2) Abraham gave tithes to Melchizedek, acknowledging his priestly authority. (3) Melchizedek's priesthood was described as unending and appeared before the Law that established the temporary Aaronic priesthood. (4) Levi—symbolically present in his ancestor Abraham—paid a tithe.

God decreed that Moses' brother, Aaron, and Aaron's descendants were to serve as priests. Men of the tribe of Levi were called as priests to assist the priests descended from Aaron. Set apart for God's service, the Levites were given *a tithe* (*a tenth*) of the people's money and produce. From this, the Levites gave a tithe to the high priests.

Jesus and Melchizedek

When Israelites sinned, the Law required that they offer a sacrifice to restore broken fellowship with God. Such sacrifices were hampered by their limitations; priests who had to make sacrifices for their own sins had no way of providing full salvation for anyone else. The Law revealed sin and provided a means of putting past sins away, but it could not produce a personal and permanent moral and spiritual change. A new kind of priesthood was necessary.

There is only one way to change the priesthood and the Law which regulated it: God's Law for Israel had to be fulfilled, and the Levitical priesthood completed. Hebrews 7:13 continues the author's argument that Jesus has fulfilled and made unnecessary the Levitical priesthood. Jesus belonged to the tribe of Judah, the royal line of king David. The Mosaic Law did not recognize anyone from Judah as qualified to serve as priest. Jesus, as priest, then, fulfills the priesthood of Melchizedek. As a descendent of David, He is the rightful king of Israel. He perfectly fulfilled the priesthood foreshadowed by Melchizedek.

Think about the fact that the Jews had a set view of the priesthood and their anticipated Messiah. Jesus did not fit that mold. Their presumption resulted in enormous loss and had eternal consequences.

We all have preconceived ideas. Scripture doesn't tell us to blindly accept what we have been taught. The Bereans were praised for examining the Scriptures to see if Paul's teaching was true. They were open to rethinking their positions, but did so thoughtfully, prayerfully, and carefully.

The eternal, entirely adequate character of the new order replaces the temporary, inadequate nature of the old order. This new priest is not chosen on the basis of ancestry. He is *"indestructible."* His death on the Cross was His choice, a sacrifice of one who, by His nature, was not subject to death. Verse 17 declares the superiority of Christ's priesthood. In verses 18-19, Christ brings a *"better hope"*—the assurance that our High Priest will bring people into God's presence. The Law only pointed out a need for change that Jesus would actually bring about.

The Superiority of Christ's Priesthood

God's *oath* makes the supremacy of Christ's priesthood doubly secure. The Greek word translated *oath* is a synonym for *mediate*. It stresses how God keeps His covenant. Jesus guarantees for us the upholding and fulfilling of this new and better covenant.

Verses 23-25 make another comparison—Levitical priests die; Jesus does not. His priesthood is permanent. He is the eternal Priest who conquered death.

Christ's intercession is personal, constant, and availing. This representative work will continue until Christ fulfills the perfecting of humanity. *"He is able"* points to the Lord's unlimited power. *"To save"* means *totally save*. Christ provides complete salvation to every person who comes to God through Him.

Think about how Jesus *"always lives to make intercession for* [you]*."* In Luke 22:32 we find Jesus interceding for Peter because Satan is about to test him. As your High Priest, Jesus is also interceding for you. What do you think He might be praying about for you?

Hebrews 7:26 points us to the superiority of Jesus. *"Holy"* sums up Christ's moral character. His sinlessness qualifyies Him as our mediator. *"Innocent"* means *blameless*. *"Unstained"* refers to the purity of life and ministry Christ carried out. *"Separated from sinners"* refers to keeping Himself holy while sharing our humanity and our company.

In His sacrifice, Jesus presented a permanent sin offering when, for our sake, He gave His life on the Cross. The *"once for all"* (7:27) of His sacrifice took away sin and need never be repeated or improved upon. Christ is both the sacrifice and the one who sacrifices. In neither the Melchizedek nor the Aaronic priesthoods was this possible.

The author ends by restating that the Levitical high priests experienced weakness, sin, and death. The High Priest after the order of Melchizedek is a Son whose work of redemption is eternally perfected; a Son who, having become man, has been raised to the throne of God.

Personalize this lesson.

✓ Jesus Christ, the fulfillment toward which Israel's history had been moving, broke in suddenly upon the fixed habits of religious people. They resisted change—even the good change God had planned. Do you ever feel like the Hebrew Christians? Is your identity threatened when you are asked to let go of an old habit, belief, or understanding?

God often seems too radical for us; He seems always to be expecting us to change. But spiritual growth involves changing behavior, attitudes, and values. *"If anyone is in Christ, he is a new creation. The old has passed away; behold, the new has come"* (2 Corinthians 5:17). Perhaps our most subtle struggle is between our natural tendency to be comfortable where we are, and our desire to make the changes God has planned for us. What do you need from God specifically to help you navigate this tension? Will you ask Him for what you need?

Lesson 10

Our Great High Priest
Hebrews 8

❖ **Hebrews 8:1-2—This Is the Reality**

   1.   How would you state the main idea of these two verses?

        _____

        _____

        _____

        _____

   2.   According to this passage, how is the ministry of Jesus unique and superior to any other?

        _____

        _____

        _____

        _____

❖ **Hebrews 8:3-5—This Is the Reflection of Reality**

   3.   Read Leviticus 9:1-7. What are the reasons for and the results of sacrifices and offerings?

        _____

        _____

        _____

        _____

        _____

4. Review Hebrews 7:26-28. How are the reasons for sacrifices and offerings fulfilled in Jesus?

_____

_____

_____

5. A *copy* is a duplicate of an original and a *shadow* is a dim reflection. What do the definitions of these words add to your understanding of verse 5? (See Exodus 25:8-9, 40.)

_____

_____

_____

❖ Hebrews 8:6—The Changes: Ministry/Covenant/Promises

6. From the following verses, what are the different aspects of Jesus' ministry?

   a. Luke 19:10 _____

   _____

   _____

   b. John 14:2-3 _____

   _____

   _____

7. From the following verses, what are the different aspects of Jesus' covenant?

   a. Romans 3:21-24_____

   _____

   _____

   b. Colossians 1:21-23 _____

   _____

   _____

8. A *mediator* is one who helps reconcile parties who are divided. What does it mean that Jesus *"mediates"* the new covenant?

    _____

    _____

❖ Hebrews 8:7-9—This Is the Problem

9. Read 8:7 with Hebrews 10:1-4. In what ways was the first covenant inadequate?

    _____

    _____

10. What is revealed about Israel in Jeremiah 7:22-28?

    _____

    _____

11. In light of how the Israelites behaved, would you expect God to make covenant promises like He did in Jeremiah 31:33-34? What does this say to you about God?

    _____

    _____

❖ Hebrews 8:10-13—This Is the Covenant

12. List four promises of the new covenant found in verse 10.

    _____

    _____

    _____

    _____

13. Which of these is most significant to you? Why?

    _____

    _____

    _____

14. Read 1 Samuel 16:7 and 2 Corinthians 3:3. What do these verses teach about the *"heart"*?

_____

_____

_____

15. What is the advantage of having God's Law written on our minds and hearts rather than on tablets of stone?

_____

_____

_____

16. At what point did the sacrificial system with its priests become obsolete? (See Matthew 27:50-52; John 19:28-30.)

_____

_____

Apply what you have learned. The Bible speaks of people whose hearts are hard, who live independently of God's leadership. Pride and intentional rebellion are often at the root of this heart-hardening, but sometimes a person's heart isn't intentionally hardened, rather it becomes calloused as a result of the pain and trauma it has experienced. Regardless of how the hardening happened, at some point all of us must make a choice: do we want to live with hard hearts, far from life-giving ways? Or will we ask Him to give us a soft heart, according to His Word in Ezekiel 36:26: *"I will give you a new heart, and a new spirit I will put within you. And I will remove the heart of stone from your flesh and give you a heart of flesh"*?

Our Great High Priest
Hebrews 8

A New and Better Covenant

After Jesus offered His sacrifice, *"He sat down at the right hand of the Majesty on high"* (Hebrews 1:3). The act of sitting signifies that His work—the forgiveness of sin and the reconciliation of people with God—was accomplished. God accepted the self-sacrifice of His Son as a full, total, and complete sacrifice. Nothing more remained to be done.

The pattern of Hebrews is to teach a greater truth by comparing it to a lesser one. Jesus serves as *"a minister in the holy places, the true tent"* (8:2). The heavenly *"holy places"* correspond to the earthly Most Holy Place, which was only a type of the greater heavenly sanctuary. As our High Priest, Jesus entered once for all into this heavenly sanctuary. *"True"* means *genuine*; however, its use does not imply that the earthly tabernacle was counterfeit. It was simply inadequate compared to the permanent and perfect place of worship God established in heaven.

Hebrews 8:3-5 further explains that Jesus is a minister of the heavenly sanctuary. The priesthood's task was to offer *"gifts and sacrifices."* If the old priesthood served as a type of Jesus and His work, then it was necessary for Him to make an offering. Jesus offered Himself.

During His earthly ministry, Jesus could not enter the Holy Place of the earthly tabernacle, for He was from the tribe of Judah. Jesus was born under the Law, so it would have been improper for Him to interfere in the service of the Levitical priests while on earth.

Built according to the *"pattern"* God gave Moses, the earthly tabernacle was a copy of the heavenly tabernacle. A *copy* suggests a duplicate, and a *shadow* implies a dim reflection of an object.

Verse 6 states that just as the new covenant is better than the old, so Christ's ministry is greater than Levi's. The Sinai covenant was established through the mediator Moses; the new and better covenant has been established through the Mediator Jesus Christ. A mediator stands between two people in a conflict or dispute to bring them together. He represents both parties. The priests mediated between God and people, but they were powerless to forge a lasting union. They were simply shadows and copies of the true Mediator who was to come.

Not only is the mediator better under the new covenant, the promises are better. Both covenants promise the knowledge of God and forgiveness of sin. However, the former *anticipates* completion while the new actually *fulfills*. In the first covenant, forgiveness sprang from what the rituals and sacrifices *represented*—a contrite heart before a gracious God. The new covenant is greatly superior because its sacrifice, the Lord Jesus Christ, actually has the power to abolish sin.

The first covenant, while not without value, *"is set aside because of its weakness and uselessness"* (7:18); its ceremonial laws could not change the human heart. Because the former covenant was faulty, another covenant was established (8:7). The blood of bulls and goats was effective only as it pointed to the true, worthy sacrifice to come, Jesus Christ.

The New Covenant Based on Superior Promises

Because of the continued failure of the Israelites to keep the covenant, God said, *"I will establish a new covenant."* However, while the *"new covenant"* was new to God's people, it was not new to God. He knew from the beginning that the Law was insufficient and that a Savior was needed. Although the prophecy speaks of the new covenant as applying to Israel and Judah, it holds a universal promise: *"They shall all know Me"* (8:11).

Verse 10 quotes from Jeremiah 31: *"I will put My laws into their minds, and write them on their hearts."* Here, the New Testament emphasis of personal renewal is first suggested. The will, which directs our actions, is influenced from the inside rather than imposed from an outside force.

The personal ministry of God's Spirit in an individual's heart results in greater revelation of God than what was available through the old covenant. God's Spirit stirs in the heart both willingness and ability to obey. A personal knowledge of God apart from the Law had to wait for a new heart, made possible by the coming of the Son. Jesus said, *"The hour is coming, and is now here, when the true worshipers will worship the Father in spirit and truth."* (John 4:23). Inward worship now replaces outward ritual.

The most important aspect of the new covenant is the total forgiveness of sins. Under the new covenant our sins are blotted out, and God chooses to remember them no longer. Only the atoning power of Jesus' blood can bury our sins in the sea of forgetfulness. Divine forgiveness—founded on grace, not works—is the high point of the New Testament.

Think about *grace*—the unearned, undeserved gift of love and forgiveness from God to wayward people. Grace is free to all who will receive it, but it was not without cost. God the Father and God the Son paid a terrible price. *"You were ransomed ... not with perishable things such as silver or gold, but with the precious blood of Christ, like that of a lamb without blemish or spot. He ... was made manifest in the last times for the sake of you who through Him are believers in God, who raised Him from the dead and gave Him glory, so that your faith and hope are in God"* (1 Peter 1:18-21).

When we accept the gift freely offered to us, our relationship with God changes. But, we must each choose for ourselves the offered privilege of being God's child. If you have not made that choice, would you prayerfully consider making that decision today? For more help, read John 3:1-17.

The new covenant is based on better promises: *"I will put My laws into their minds,"* *"they shall all know Me,"* *"I will remember their sins no more."* The words *new covenant* imply that the old covenant has fulfilled its purpose. Obsolete, it will soon disappear. God has done something new in Christ. The temple sacrifices would soon end. It is far more blessed, to live in the light of the second and better covenant, where peace dwells in one's heart, the moral nature is renewed, and death holds no fear.

Personalize this lesson.

The central thought in chapter 8 is that in Jesus Christ, God has given His people better things. With the privilege of experiencing a better Mediator, better promises, and a better covenant, there are responsibilities. God calls us to leave our spiritual childhood behind as we embrace the new covenant and go on to maturity in Christ. We can know God and know right from wrong. And we can know the joy, not only of being forgiven, but of having the power to live in a way that is pleasing to God. In what way would you like to "grow up" this week? Talk to God about it and ask for His power to change.

The Old and the New Covenants
Hebrews 9

❖ **Hebrews 9:1-5—The Former Place**

1. Read about the origins of the tabernacle in Exodus 24:13–25:9.

   a. How was the contribution of building materials initiated?

   _____

   _____

   b. How was the design of the tabernacle determined?

   _____

   _____

2. Give a brief account of these items mentioned in verse 4:

   a. the *"golden urn holding the manna"* (Exodus 16:32-34)

   _____

   _____

   b. *"Aaron's staff that budded"* (Numbers 17:1-10)

   _____

   _____

   c. *"the tablets of the covenant"* (Deuteronomy 10:1-5)

   _____

   _____

❖ Hebrews 9:6-10—The Former Practice

3. Read Leviticus 16:29–17:14.

    a. What main regulations established for Israel do you find in this Leviticus passage?

    _____

    _____

    b. God Himself instituted the sacrificial system. Why is *blood* essential to the sacrifice (17:11)?

    _____

    _____

4. According to Hebrews 9:9, what is the offering of gifts and sacrifices unable to do?

    _____

    _____

5. Review Hebrews 8:10-13. *"The time of reformation"* (9:10) is the new covenant initiated by Christ. What does it provide that *"regulations for the body"* lack?

    _____

    _____

❖ Hebrews 9:11-14—The Final Presentation

6. From this passage, record the ways in which Christ's service and sacrifice as High Priest are superior to the rituals performed by former high priests.

    _____

    _____

    _____

7. Read Isaiah 29:13; Matthew 23:23-28. What are *"dead works"*?

    _____

    _____

8. From this passage, what is the effect of having a cleansed conscience?

_____

_____

9. What does it mean to you to *"serve the living God"*?

_____

_____

_____

_____

❖ **Hebrews 9:15-22—The Fixed Price**

10. Since its beginning, the book of Hebrews has emphasized *"new"* or *"better"* things. From 9:18-22, what has not changed or been improved upon?

_____

_____

11. What is your honest reaction to the fact that the forgiveness of sin requires the shedding of blood? Talk to God about your answer, and if you need His help in understanding or accepting His ways, ask Him for it. Remember Hebrews 4:16 as you pray.

_____

_____

_____

_____

❖ **Hebrews 9:23-28—The Future Attained**

12. What phrases do you find in chapter 9 that repeat themes already presented in earlier chapters of Hebrews?

_____

_____

_____

13. On the basis of what Christ has already accomplished, is there anything that still needs to be done to provide salvation? Cite the verse that supports your answer.

_____

_____

14. How many times does a person die? Why is this truth significant in our pluralistic culture?

_____

_____

15. What does a person face upon dying? What does this imply about "second chances" after death?

_____

_____

16. How can a person ensure that his or her eternal future is secure?

_____

_____

Apply what you have learned. In one brief chapter, we see that things of the past bear great influence on the present. This is true in our personal lives—we are molded by our past. How does your past influence your present (and future)? Thank God for the blessings that have made your present good. Ask Him to redeem and show you the purpose for the difficult things so that they, too, can be part of a blessed present and future.

The Old and the New Covenants
Hebrews 9

The writer has compared the priesthoods of Aaron and Jesus, the two covenants, and now contrasts the two tabernacles.

The Temporary Levitical Sacrifices

The tabernacle's structure and pattern of service proclaimed its temporary character. It was *"earthly"* (9:1), literally, *manmade*. The Holy Place was the place of daily priestly work. This outermost room contained a golden *"lampstand"* and a wooden table overlaid with gold. The table was used for pouring out offerings, and, every Sabbath, 12 fresh cakes were placed on it. The innermost room, *"the Most Holy Place,"* was set apart by a curtain.

The golden altar of incense is included in the Most Holy Place, although Exodus 30:6 and Leviticus 16:18 locate it in the Holy Place. Possibly, the writer is picturing the tent on the Day of Atonement. The gold-covered Ark of the Covenant, placed permanently in the Most Holy Place, contained a golden urn of manna, Aaron's staff, and the stone tablets inscribed with the Law. On the gold lid, or mercy seat, were the golden cherubim. Between their wings, God met with His people. On the Day of Atonement, blood was sprinkled there for the people's sin.

God established the Day of Atonement as a national day of repentance. Sins separate people from God; without a means of purification, they have no way to approach Him. Annually, following the prescribed ritual, a priest entered God's holy presence to make atonement for sin—but *"not without taking blood"* (9:7). The Day of Atonement provided ceremonial cleansing and instruction. The Holy Spirit was showing that this tabernacle did not provide a direct way for all to come into God's presence.

The old system illustrates what the faithful awaited. As God had planned, Levitical rituals held a nation together in His name, taught of His holiness and mercy, and foreshadowed the blood sacrifice of God's own Son. The illustration points to *"the present age,"* during which Jesus' sacrifice brought pardon and renewal to all who believe. Jewish ritual was good and familiar, but temporary. Readers are reminded of the superiority of the new order ushered in by Christ.

Think about how, as a man, Jesus was approachable, and by His death, He made God approachable. Jesus' death on the Cross opened the way to God for anyone who accepts Him by faith. Instead of waiting outside while a priest goes in, we are encouraged to enter His presence boldly. Christians are made holy inwardly by the cleansing power of Jesus' blood. Then, through the Holy Spirit, we show the world what He is like. As the tabernacle and its furnishings symbolized the coming Savior, we represent the Savior who has come. *"Therefore, we are ambassadors for Christ, God making His appeal through us"* (2 Corinthians 5:20).

Christ, the Eternal, Heavenly Sacrifice

Verse 11 expands Jesus' title: *"high priest of the good things that have come."* The good things that can be experienced now are close fellowship with God and His people, the Law written on hearts and minds, the hope of the Lord's return for His people, and the remission of sin.

Christ's work as High Priest is immeasurably superior to the old system, first because it is accomplished in the heavenly tabernacle. Jesus said a temple *"not made with hands"* would replace the Jerusalem temple. It is a spiritual temple—the very dwelling place of God.

Second, Christ obtained redemption by accomplishing what Aaron and his successors *illustrated.* The high priests sacrificed repeatedly before God, but Christ's sacrifice was perfect and eternal. Christ's blood removes the defiling power of sin and its dead works—it makes things new: *"If anyone is in Christ, he is a new creation. The old has passed away; behold, the new has come"* (2 Corinthians 5:17). The phrase *"through the eternal Spirit offered Himself"* (Hebrews 9:14) portrays Jesus, by the power of the Holy Spirit, yielding His life to God as a guilt offering.

Christ, Mediator of a New Covenant

Jesus, as Mediator, is now connected to the new covenant by the shedding of His blood. The Lord expressed this when passing the cup at the Last Supper: *"This is My blood of the covenant"* (Mark 14:24). Where Christ serves and how He provides redemption are new, as is the result of this transaction. Those who respond to His call receive a new inheritance.

A will does not take effect until the one who made it dies. Once death occurs, the will cannot be changed. God gave to the Jews an eternal inheritance in the form of a covenant or will, but *"not even the first covenant was inaugurated without blood"* (Hebrews 9:18).

The Law represents all that God revealed to Moses. Shed blood and the sacrifice of innocent animals emphasized the seriousness of sin. Verse 19 describes how Moses sprinkled blood on the altar and on the people. Water increased the quantity of fluid. Hyssop, or wild marjoram stalk, was wound with scarlet wool to act as a sponge. The blood of animal sacrifices was central to the old covenant: *"Without the shedding of blood there is no forgiveness of sins,"* reminding offenders that their self-effort and remorse were not enough against sin.

Christ, the Sufficient Offering for Sin

In verses 25-26, the high point of Hebrews has been reached: *"He has appeared once for all."* No longer must multiple offerings for sin be made. When Christ sacrificed Himself, He did away with sin. If His offering had not been sufficient to atone for the sins of the whole world, then it would have to be repeated. However, its effectiveness penetrated all time and completely satisfied all requirements. Christ presented Himself before God *"once for all at the end of the ages"* (9:26)—the climax of history.

In 9:27-28, the author states that people die once, and judgment follows. Christ, too, became a man and accepted the requirement of death. But death is not the final chapter. The Lord *"will appear a second time"*—not to deal with sin, for that has already been done—but *"to save those who are eagerly waiting for Him."* All that Christ has achieved for His people by sacrificing Himself will be theirs to enjoy forever.

Personalize this lesson.

"Without the shedding of blood there is no forgiveness of sins" (Hebrews 9:22). The blood of every animal sacrificed on the altar foreshadowed the blood of the supremely innocent sacrifice—Jesus Christ, the Son of God. *"Behold,"* John the Baptist said, *"the Lamb of God, who takes away the sin of the world!"* (John 1:29). God has provided the only acceptable offering for sin. Jesus paid sin's penalty and freed us from its bondage. We are not just excused—we are forgiven.

Lesson 12

Christ's Finished Work
Hebrews 10:1-18

❖ **Hebrews 10:1-4—The Problem Is a Shadow**

1. What are *"the good things"* spoken of in Hebrews 9:11 and 10:1?

    _____

    _____

    _____

2. From this passage, list at least three weaknesses in the Law.

    _____

    _____

    _____

3. Read Galatians 3:23-24. What profitable purpose did the Law serve?

    _____

    _____

❖ **Hebrews 10:5-7—The Answer Is the Son**

4. How do the following verses distinguish the sacrifice of Jesus from all others?

    a. John 1:12

    _____

    _____

    b.   Romans 5:11

_____

_____

    c.   Philippians 2:5-8

_____

_____

5. What connection do you see between Luke 4:14-21 and Hebrews 10:7?

_____

_____

❖ Hebrews 10:8-10—The Lesson Concerns Surrender

6. a.   What is *"the first"* that God *"does away with"* (10:9)? (See also Hebrews 7:12, 18-19; 8:7, 13.)

_____

_____

    b.   What is *"the second"*?

_____

_____

7. For what purposes were *"the first"* things surrendered?

_____

_____

8. What do the following passages reveal about the cost of Christ's sacrificial surrender?

    a.   Luke 23:20-25

_____

_____

    b.   Luke 23:32-37

_____

_____

9. Read Luke 22:42. What did Jesus surrender that we also are called to surrender?

_____

_____

_____

❖ Hebrews 10:11-14—The Solution Involves Sacrifice

10. Read 1 Peter 2:4-5, 9. Who are the priests Peter addresses in these verses?

_____

_____

11. According to Romans 12:1 and Hebrews 13:15-16, what spiritual sacrifices are priests to offer?

_____

_____

_____

12. Concerning Hebrews 10:12-13:

    a.   What has been done?

_____

_____

    b.   What remains to be done?

_____

_____

_____

❖ Hebrews 10:15-18—The Confirmation Concerns the Spirit

13. What does 2 Peter 1:19-21 teach about the words of God's prophets?

14. What tasks of the Holy Spirit are described in John 14:25-26?

15. Following the summary of the new covenant (Hebrews 10:16-17), what conclusion does the author reach?

16. Why is there *"no longer any offering for sin"*?

Apply what you have learned. Verse 16 talks about the difference between having God's laws available externally (on tablets, in books) and internally (in hearts, written on minds). Why is having God's laws in our hearts and minds better than having to read or hear it? How can you participate with the Holy Spirit in this process of making God's truth internal?

Christ's Finished Work
Hebrews 10:1-18

The Law Is a Shadow

"The law" (10:1) often refers to the whole Old Testament system of worship. In its strictest sense, however, it refers to the Law of Moses or the first five books of the Bible (Genesis through Deuteronomy). *"A shadow"* suggests the reality that casts it. Here, the reality is personal access to God and all else that the new covenant brings.

"Of the good things to come" points to the benefits of Christ's new covenant, just as 9:11 had. Now, as the apostle Paul says, *"Christ is the end of the law"* (Romans 10:4). We see a progression in the way God revealed Himself to humanity. First came the Law of Moses, then the gospel of Christ, and ultimately the fullest reality in the heavens. A worshiper of Jesus enjoys the fulfillment of the good things promised in the Old Testament and anticipates even greater things to come.

"The same sacrifices that are continually offered every year" (Hebrews 10:1) were powerless to cleanse the conscience of God's people. This system of worship waited for its perfection in a sacrifice that would go beyond ceremony and actually cleanse the inner person, once for all.

"In these sacrifices there is a reminder of sins every year" (10:3). They provided ceremonial purity, or *"external"* cleansing. They educated and prepared the people's faith for the coming of Christ, when their true meaning would be seen.

Christ, the Once-for-All Sacrifice

Embedded in the Law of Moses was the teaching of the temporary nature of animal sacrifices. In Psalm 40, which the author of Hebrews quotes from, the psalmist speaks of his realization that God demands willing obedience to His commands. He approaches Psalm 40 in its Messianic, or prophetic, sense and sees the psalmist's words as an expression of the mind of the incarnate Son of God on His coming into the world. The writer thus reads in the light that is shed by the New Testament, and in these lines of David, rightly hears the voice of Christ.

Hebrews 10:5-6 states that animal sacrifices and meat and drink offerings are not primarily what God seeks—and they never were: *"To obey is better than sacrifice, and to listen than the fat of rams"* (1 Samuel 15:22). God appointed the sacrifices to provide the way for people to live in holiness. He wanted fellowship with an obedient people. While the sacrifices and offerings were divinely commanded, and failure to offer them would be disobedience, they were not the final will and fully formed purpose of God.

By the time of the prophets, the people knew that God sought a person's heart, not a ceremonial, habitual performance. Psalm 40:8 is quoted: *"I have come to do Your will."* The Messiah, of His own volition, presents Himself to do God's will. Hebrews 9:26 further asserts that the obedience of Christ to the will of His Father necessitated His voluntary self-sacrifice. The next sentence, *"He does away with the first in order to establish the second"* (Hebrews 10:9), may be paraphrased this way: "God does away with all the old sacrifices and authorizes in their place the ultimate sacrifice of Christ."

Through the offering of Jesus, *"we have been sanctified ... once for all."* Christ's sacrifice secures the justification of His people and sets them apart for God. It was God's will that the inferior sacrifice should give way to the sacrifice of the Son. It is also God's will that His people be holy.

Think about what it means to be *"sanctified through the offerings of the body of Jesus Christ."* The word *holy*, when describing the Father, the Son, and the Holy Spirit, denotes *absolute purity, goodness,* and *righteousness.* But when it refers to people or things, *holy* [*sanctified*] means *separated* or *dedicated to God.* This holiness is spiritual and God-ordained; it is not self-attained. God declares, *"Be holy, for I the LORD your God am holy"* (Leviticus 19:2). In our spiritual nature, we are made holy.

In our behavior, we are commanded to be holy. Our
attitudes and actions should reflect the holiness that God
has planted within each of us at the moment of our personal
spiritual rebirth.

Evidence of Christ's Finished Work

Again, the writer emphasizes that God's purpose for sacrifice is the
removal of sins. The Levitical priest repeatedly offers the same sacrifices
because his offerings do not take away sins. In contrast, by one offering,
Christ Jesus accomplished His work, and His sacrifice removed sin. His
perfect high priesthood and His intercession as High Priest remained.
The need for further sacrifice ceased.

Sanctification comes to God's people, but complete defeat comes to all
His unyielding enemies—the devil, the power of death, and those who
reject Christ. By His one sacrifice, Jesus did all that is or ever will be
necessary to provide forgiveness and to achieve the perfection of human
character. In this life, no one is free from all sin, but ultimately our
perfection will be achieved and revealed.

It may be difficult for believers today, who are centuries and cultures
removed from animal sacrifices, to appreciate the weight of this
message. For 1st-century believers, however, their entire life experience
revolved around the annual calendar of sacrifices. When Jesus made
atonement for sin, the entire sacrificial system was rendered obsolete.
Jewish Christians, therefore, were released from obligation to the Old
Testament sacrificial system. This would produce great relief. But, the
loss of what was familiar could also produce a yearning for "the old way"
and thus endanger faith.

Personalize this lesson.

It's normal to monitor growth. So, it's not surprising that we try to measure our spiritual growth—usually in terms of our feelings. The New Testament deals little with how we *feel* and mostly with how we *behave.* Jesus pleased His Father by saying, *"I have come to do Your will, O God"* (10:7). We can please Him the very same way. Why not ask your heavenly Father—right now, in whatever circumstances you find yourself—to help you to act in line with the things you believe to be true about Him?

A Call To Persevere
Hebrews 10:19-39

Memorize God's Word: Hebrews 10:23-24

❖ Hebrews 10:19-22—Let Us Be Strong in Worship

1. List the three aspects in verses 19-21 by which we have
    confidence to enter God's presence.

    a. _____

    _____

    b. _____

    _____

    c. _____

    _____

2. How would you explain to someone what it means to *"draw
    near"* to God (10:22)?

    _____

    _____

❖ Hebrews 10:23-25—Let Us Benefit One Another

3. Review Hebrews 10:17-18. What is our *"hope,"* spoken of in
    verse 23, based on?

    _____

    _____

4. *"Let us"* is used three times in 10:22-24 as the author exhorts his readers to various actions. Choose the one that is most important to you. If you were to follow through on this exhortation, what difference would it make in your life?

    _____

    _____

    _____

❖ Hebrews 10:26-31—Let Us Beware of Rejecting Truth

5. Review Hebrews 3:12 and 6:4-8. In light of these verses, what kind of sin is addressed in verses 26-31?

    _____

    _____

6. According to the following verses, what aspects of God's character are revealed when He deals with sin other than apostasy?

    a. Hebrews 2:17-18_____

    _____

    b. Hebrews 4:15-16_____

    _____

    c. Hebrews 5:2_____

    _____

7. What behaviors lead to judgment, according to 10:26-31?

    _____

    _____

8. Why is the punishment referred to in Hebrews 10:29 greater than that in 10:28?

    _____

    _____

    _____

9. From 2 Peter 2:4-9, what is the key to avoiding God's wrath?

_____

_____

❖ Hebrews 10:32-34—Let Us Bear Up With Hope

10. After his warnings in verses 26-31, how does the author encourage his readers?

_____

_____

11. How do these verses encourage you?

_____

_____

12. What do you learn about *"a better possession and an abiding one"* (10:34) from Matthew 6:19-20?

_____

_____

_____

13. Would you say it is easy or difficult to appreciate *"a better possession and a lasting one"*? Explain your answer.

_____

_____

❖ Hebrews 10:35-39—Let Us Believe and Be Saved

14. State from verses 35-36:

   a. The responsibilities of the believer_____

_____

_____

   b. The responses of God_____

_____

_____

15. What does *"shrinks back"* (10:38) mean to you?

_____

_____

16. In verse 39, what is the alternative to "shrinking back"?

_____

_____

17. What can you apply from this passage to warn and encourage those around you?

_____

_____

_____

_____

Apply what you have learned. Hebrews 10 is written to *"stir"* the readers to love and good works. The manner in which we do this "stirring" is important. Is there someone you know who needs encouragement toward love and good works? What might be a helpful way for you to do this? What would be an unhelpful way? If you think God is prompting you to encourage someone, make sure you also seek Him for a way to do it that will help and not discourage that person.

A Call To Persevere
Hebrews 10:19-39

Confidence and Perseverance

"Therefore" refers to the preceding section of teaching. Now, steadfastness becomes the focus. The author's use of the words *"brothers"* and *"we"* emphasizes his identification with them.

For believers there is no need for uncertainty when drawing near to God. The Most Holy Place has been opened. We enter *"by the new and living way that He opened"*—through Jesus Christ, who is the only way into the presence of the Father. *"Living"* may also mean enduring, in contrast to the temporary rituals of the past. This new way goes through the curtain that is Christ's own body (*"through His flesh"*), which was offered, once for all, as the perfect, eternal sacrifice.

The author suggests that the tearing of Christ's flesh is similar to the tearing of the temple curtain at the time of the Crucifixion. Christ's death provides direct access into God's presence. We also *"have a great priest,"* superior to any former high priest because He is the Son of God. *"The house of God"* signifies the family, or kingdom, made up of all God's people.

Without hesitation, we are urged to *"draw near."* However, one needs to have a sincere and honest heart full of faith to draw near effectively. We are prepared to do this through the internal work of God (purified hearts, 9:14) and the outward sign (the washing of our bodies), probably baptism. Because of what Jesus has done for us, we are to draw near to God with the assurance of faith.

Verse 23 urges steadfastness based on God's faithful and trustworthy Word. What Christians believe, and the hope that is a part of that belief, may be held firmly because God's faithful character is never in doubt. Thus we are to urge each other on to Christian conduct.

Spiritual maturity and steadfastness grow through worshiping together, but some were neglecting these gatherings. Loss of love and a weakened spiritual resolve result. Christians need each other, especially *"as you see the Day drawing near"*—a reference to the final coming of the Lord and the judgment to follow. Love and good deeds must be the activities of God's people until that Day.

Think about the reality of Christ's return. The early church expected His return any day. Jesus' own teaching about His return stresses our duty to be ready for His coming, which means being busy doing His will. We must expect Him to return momentarily—and be faithful as we wait. Consider Jesus' words: *"You also must be ready, for the Son of Man is coming at an hour you do not expect"* (Luke 12:40). Are you ready?

Warning Against Apostasy

The warnings in Hebrews 6:4-8 and 10:26-31 are meant to guard against apostasy by revealing the nature of this sin and its fatal results. If people *"deliberately"* reject God's love, they are left to face His judgment. To *"go on sinning deliberately"* (10:26) refers to a willful abandonment of the truth after it has been received. If a person rejects the sacrifice of Christ, his situation is hopeless for *"there is no other name under heaven"* (Acts 4:12) by which salvation is obtained.

For those who reject Jesus to the end, there is no further opportunity for salvation—only *"a fearful expectation of judgment."* If physical death was the punishment for deliberately offending the Law of Moses, how much greater must be the consequence for rejecting the new covenant, instituted by Jesus. The *apostate*, then, is one who tramples underfoot God's Son, regarding with contempt the Prophet and Priest of the new covenant; one who counts the blood of the covenant a common or unholy thing, and who *"has outraged the Spirit of grace"* (Hebrews 10:29). These words do not refer to one who is weak in the faith, but to one who knows what it means to walk with God, yet willfully throws aside salvation.

To support the idea that judgment is no idle threat, the writer appeals to knowledge of God's character and quotes from Scripture. Deuteronomy

32:35 declares God's right to punish: *"Vengeance is Mine ."* The second quotation is found in Deuteronomy 32:36 and Psalm 135:14: *"The LORD will vindicate* [judge] *His people."* Only two verdicts are possible: *acquitted*—in the name of Jesus, or *condemned*—to the wrath of God that is against sin. Verse 31 describes this fearful reality.

The Reward for Those Who Endure

Wisely, then, the writer encourages his readers to renewed endurance by recalling their former experiences. Hebrews 10:32 states that their past courage deserves commendation and should be a steadying force to them now. Some of these Jewish Christians had undergone persecution after they had been *"enlightened"* (10:32). They had suffered public disgrace, affliction, and loss of property. Believing and suffering went hand-in-hand.

The theme of encouragement continues as the author adapts Habakkuk 2:3-4, *"The vision awaits its appointed time; ... it will surely come; ... but the righteous shall live by his faith."* The Hebrew language used by Habakkuk refers to a vision or revelation, but the Greek encourages a strong Messianic interpretation: *"the coming one will come"* (Hebrews 10:37). Christ will soon appear. The fulfillment of the promise is not far off: *"yet a little while."* His name is still *"the coming one,"* for as He once came in the flesh, He is coming again in power and great glory.

When the writer of Hebrews says, *"My righteous one shall live by faith"* (10:38), he turns his attention to a complementary thought—God's people will live according to faith. Faith and faithfulness are rooted in God's faithfulness to us. *"If he shrinks back, My soul has no pleasure in him"* presents a warning. The verb means to turn oneself back in a cowardly way. Clearly, God enables the believer to stand, thus the believer must choose to stand.

The author is confident of his readers' eventual victory. He uses the personal pronoun *"we"* in speaking of those who do not shrink back but *"have faith and preserve in their souls."* The emphasis is positive. If they are true to their faith and take advantage of all the resources that God has provided, they will endure their present crisis without falling.

Personalize this lesson.

By nature most of us are not patient or persevering. But patience is a fruit of the Spirit—something God will produce in us if we allow Him to. In fact, three aspects of the fruit of the Spirit will help us persevere in hardship: patience, faithfulness, and self-control. What do you need from God in order to persevere in the circumstances you are challenged by today? Ask Him for it—and believe that He will help you.

Lesson 14

Those Who Exercise Faith, Part 1
Hebrews 11:1-22

Memorize God's Word: Hebrews 11:1

❖ Hebrews 11:1-3—The Perspective of Faith

1. According to the following verses, in what can we put our hope and by so doing, assure our faith?

   a. Psalm 119:74 _____

   _____

   b. Psalm 147:11 _____

   _____

   c. Titus 1:1-2 _____

   _____

   d. 1 John 3:2-3 _____

   _____

2. Using a dictionary, define the following words:

   a. *assurance* _____

   _____

   b. *conviction* _____

   _____

3. Write a description of what *faith* means to you.

   _____

   _____

❖ Hebrews 11:4-7—The Potential of Faith

4. What phrases in 11:4 suggest the difference between the sacrifices of Abel and those of Cain?

   _____

   _____

   _____

5. Even though Abel died, how does he still speak?

   _____

   _____

6. What does this suggest about the potential of a person's faith?

   _____

   _____

7. How did God reward Enoch's faith?

   _____

   _____

8. According to the last half of verse 6, why is it impossible to please God without faith?

   _____

   _____

9. Read Genesis 6:5-8.

   a. What were the conditions on earth like during the time Noah lived?

      _____

      _____

   b. How does Noah's life encourage you in the times in which you live?

      _____

      _____

      _____

❖ Hebrews 11:8-12—The Pressing On in Faith

10. Record the phrases in this passage that show that Abraham faced the unknown.

_____

_____

_____

11. From Romans 4:20-21, how did Abraham maintain his faith?

_____

_____

_____

12. What do we learn from Hebrews 12:22-24 and Revelation 21:22-27 about *"the city"* Abraham anticipated in faith?

_____

_____

_____

❖ Hebrews 11:13-16—The Patience of Faith

13. When the things you are hoping for by faith seem to be far off, what encouragement can you take from this passage?

_____

_____

_____

14. What attitudes about your life would change if you were to think of yourself as a *"stranger and exile on the earth"*?

_____

_____

_____

❖ Hebrews 11:17-22—The Passing On of Faith

15. From the example of Abraham and Isaac, what kind of tests of faith might we expect?

_____

_____

_____

16. How do the examples of the faithful people in this passage confirm the definition of faith in 11:1?

_____

_____

17. How, specifically, do these verses challenge or encourage you?

_____

_____

_____

_____

_____

Apply what you have learned. The author of Hebrews directs us to consider generation after generation of people who persevered by faith. We dare not minimize the significance of such examples. The effects of faith impact history and have the power to influence our lives today. Thank God for those who walked with God before you. Ask Him to help you follow in their footsteps, leaving a well-marked path for others to follow.

Those Who Exercise Faith, Part 1
Hebrews 11:1-22

The Meaning of Faith

Faith is portrayed in this chapter as a firm belief that God will carry
out His promises in spite of seemingly contrary circumstances. The
emphasis of faith is not on the internal attitude of the people mentioned
but on their active response to God's truth. Faith gives us an inner
assurance that the unseen world and unrealized promises of God are
true. Then, the reality or actual substance of these promises is fulfilled by
actions. Faith has its solid basis in God's Word. Our confidence rests on
and our actions are motivated by God's authority.

The Creation account in Genesis support this definition. No human
witnessed the creation of the world; yet, by faith, we accept that
God spoke and it was done. Verse 3 indicates that God did not work
with previously existing material; rather, by His Word, He created
the physical universe. Science can only speculate about the cause or
source of all that exists. Various scientific theories about the origin of
the universe start with pre-existing substance—a mixture of gases, for
example. This is the mystery of "first cause" that makes scientists wonder
and that draws Christians to the Word of God.

Men of Faith Before the Flood

More than 15 times in the coming verses, the sentence begins *"By faith."*
In the first example, Abel presents a sacrifice acceptable to God, while
his brother Cain does not. The argument is this: Cain somehow resisted
God's direction and turned from His revealed will. This is made clear by
Genesis 4:7: *"If you do well, will you not be accepted?"* Abel is an example
of one whose actions were consistent with his understanding of God.
The account in Genesis does not specify how Abel's sacrifice was better

than Cain's; however, we do see that it is not the ritual of sacrifice that pleases God, but the heart of the giver.

Enoch, because of his faith, was taken to heaven without dying. The author emphasizes, by contrast, that it is impossible to please God without faith. Two beliefs are needed to draw near to God. First, one must believe that *"God is."* Second, that God *"rewards those who earnestly seek Him"* (11:6). A person with God-pleasing faith strongly seeks Him, believing that He will respond and make Himself known.

Noah proved his faith by building the ark when there was no sign of a coming flood. Noah believed God's warning of coming judgment. His faith enabled him to obey, in spite of being misunderstood by others. The statement that he *"in reverent fear built an ark"* reveals Noah's faith. Noah is the earliest person in Scripture to be called *righteous*. The other people of Noah's time had the same warnings but did not listen. The their disbelief and disobedience contrasts to Noah's faith.

Abraham and Sarah's Faith

The first evidence of Abraham's great faith is seen when God calls him *"to go out to a place"* He promised to give him. On God's promise alone, Abraham set out for a destination specified only as *"the land that I will show you"* (Genesis 12:1). This is exactly what faith demands. Confidence in God's word moves us willingly toward the unknown. While Abraham's faith kept him steadfast, he did not possess the land God promised him, except for a burial plot. Isaac and Jacob died without receiving the Promised Land as their own, but they still believed in the promise.

Through Abraham, the author begins teaching of an eternal city *"whose designer and builder is God."* The second example of Abraham's faith has to do with God's promise of descendants. Abraham relied on God's promise, and this trust enabled him to accomplish what was humanly impossible. Despite old age and barrenness, Sarah and Abraham had a son, Isaac. Through Isaac came an abundance of offspring.

Faith for a Better Country

The author elaborates further on heaven in Hebrews 11:13-16. Abraham, Sarah, and their descendants died in faith as they had lived in faith. They were not at home on the earth. The patriarchs knew God personally and anticipated everlasting fellowship with Him. God rewards those who earnestly seek Him, and so He honors them by calling Himself *"the God of Abraham, the God of Isaac, and the God of Jacob"* (Exodus 3:6).

Think about how God revealed Himself progressively to Israel. He gave the fullest revelation of Himself and life after death through Jesus Christ. People of the Old Testament looked forward to the future, as Psalm 49:15 shows: *"God will ransom my soul from the power of Sheol, for He will receive me."* The patriarchs believed that the city prepared for them was a better place than this earth. Because of the Incarnation, we can be certain that we will experience eternal life in heaven.

Anticipating the Promises

The author emphasizes Abraham's unshakable faith in God's promises as he focuses on the time God ordered Abraham to offer Isaac as a sacrifice. Abraham obediently took Isaac to the place of sacrifice. He reasoned that if Isaac died, God would resurrect him. Figuratively speaking, Abraham did receive Isaac back from the dead, for Abraham was holding the knife in midair when he heard the heavenly command to stop.

Isaac accepted the overruling of his own purpose (Genesis 27:33-40) and *"by faith"* bestowed blessings on both sons for their futures. The certainty that God was Lord over all, even the tactics of deception, made Isaac a model of the *"the people of old "* who were commended for their faith (Hebrews 11:2).

Jacob (later renamed *Israel*), unlike his father, was neither confused nor deceived when he acted contrary to prevailing social practices. He purposely blessed Joseph's son Ephraim, though he was younger than his brother Manasseh (Genesis 48:11-20), just as he, the younger son, had been chosen above Esau.

Joseph made his brothers promise to take his bones back to Canaan, even though none of Abraham's descendants lived in the Promised Land at that time. Joseph's faith in God withstood separation from his family, slavery in Egypt, years in prison, and eventual honor as Pharaoh's second-in-command. Neither hardship nor success dimmed his faith in God's promises.

Personalize this lesson.

✓ We see in this lesson many examples of how faith leads to obedience, which in turn leads to deeper knowledge of God. Just like the men and women in ancient Israel had to get to know God step by step as they moved along in their journeys of faith, so do we. Often we begin our life in Christ with false ideas about God. We might think of Him as distant or overbearing, punitive, or indulging. Like Abraham, we need a greater understanding of God's ways. Every step of faith and obedience opens us up to knowing more of His love, more of His grace, more of His power and mercy. How have your steps of faith and obedience caused your view of God and knowledge of Him to grow?

Those Who Exercise Faith, Part 2
Hebrews 11:23-40

❖ **Hebrews 11:23-26—Faith Sees Beyond What Is Physical**

1. Read Exodus 2:1-10 and Acts 7:17-22. What, by faith, did Moses' parents experience and accomplish?

_____

_____

_____

2. What encouragement for parents do you see in Proverbs 22:6 and Hebrews 11:24-25?

_____

_____

_____

❖ **Hebrews 11:27-29—Faith Sees the Unseen**

3. Read Exodus 3:1-12. What experience helped prepare Moses for his return to Egypt?

_____

_____

4. What did Moses have to do before he could receive a sign that God had sent him (3:10-12)?

_____

_____

5. What visible symbols did God use to lead the Israelites? (See
    Exodus 13:21-22.)

    _____

    _____

6. Read Exodus 14:10-16, 21-22. Record what the Israelites had to
    do in order to be rescued.

    _____

    _____

    _____

❖ Hebrews 11:30-31—Faith Demands That We Take Risks

7. Read the story of Jericho in Joshua 6:1-20. What risks (emo-
    tional, physical, and spiritual) did the Israelites experienced at
    Jericho when they chose to obey God?

    _____

    _____

    _____

    _____

8. What risks do you sometimes take when you choose to obey
    God?

    _____

    _____

    _____

9. a. Read Joshua 2:1-16. How much did Rahab know about God
        before demonstrating confidence in Him (2:8-11)?

        _____

        _____

    b. How did she demonstrate her faith (2:4, 12-16)?

        _____

        _____

   c. According to Joshua 6:22-25, how was her faith rewarded?

_____

_____

❖ Hebrews 11:32-35—Faith Can Conquer

10. What other victorious deeds done *"through faith"* are mentioned in these verses?

_____

_____

11. What character qualities do you see in the people mentioned here who demonstrated such great faith?

_____

_____

12. Read the following verses that talk about the kind of faith that overcomes: Joshua 1:9; Psalm 118:5-9; John 16:33. What encouragement do you receive from these verses?

_____

_____

_____

_____

❖ Hebrews 11:36-40—Faith Can Be Costly

13. This passage discusses physical and emotional abuses committed against people of faith. Is there a Bible character (from Hebrews 11 or elsewhere in Scripture) whose example of costly faith gives you courage? Who did you choose, and how does this person's life encourage you?

_____

_____

_____

_____

14. Hebrews 11:39-40 speaks of God's promises that are to be fulfilled in Christ. What specific promises do you find in the following verses?

   a. Matthew 5:10-12 _____

       _____

       _____

   b. Luke 18:29-30 _____

       _____

       _____

   c. John 14:2-3 _____

       _____

       _____

15. How do the passages you've just read help you better understand the relationship between God's deliverance and a person's faith?

       _____

       _____

       _____

       _____

Apply what you have learned. Faith is not human courage or sharpened intellect. And it is never perfect. Even people of the greatest faith are limited by human frailties—mistakes, sin, sorrow, and loss. Faith is simply trusting God and living out that trust, whether the day brings disappointments or joy. Faith knows that in all things God works for our eventual and ultimate good. What opportunities do you have today to exercise your faith in who God is?

Those Who Exercise Faith, Part 2
Hebrews 11:23-40

Moses, God's Chosen Leader

At the time of Moses' birth, the reigning Pharaoh had tried to limit
the increasing number of Israelites in Egypt: He ordered midwives to
kill every Jewish male at birth. Nevertheless, with the birth of their
son, Moses' parents responded to this decree with an act of faith.
Recognizing that *"he was no ordinary child"* (11:23, NIV), they risked
their lives to save him. Somehow, Moses' parents understood that God
had a special work for their child to do. How they were able to hide him
for three months we do not know. What we do know is that their faith,
not fear of consequences, controlled their conduct.

As an adult, Moses *"refused to be called the son of Pharaoh's daughter"*
(11:24), and established his own faith in the God of Israel. Moved by
compassion for the Hebrew plight, he rejected *"the fleeting pleasures of
sin"* (11:25). By faith, Moses instituted the Passover.

Moses Encourages the Israelites

When Moses and his people arrived at the Red Sea, Pharaoh and his
army were close behind. The people were terrified, angry, and faithless.
But Moses' faith inspired them. He said, *"Fear not, stand firm, and see
the salvation of the LORD, which He will work for you today. . . . The LORD
will fight for you, and you have only to be silent"* (Exodus 14:13-14). The
Israelites believed God's promise of deliverance and God saved them.

The Conquest of Canaan

Hebrews 11:30 refers to the generation who followed Joshua into
Canaan. Their faith brought them victory at Jericho. Joshua believed
God's instructions and inspired the people to march around Jericho.

The Israelites risked everything, even their national reputation, as they placed their trust in God.

Rahab, a Canaanite prostitute, is esteemed for her faith, although she comes from a pagan, idolatrous culture. The people of Jericho feared the Israelites because of their victories in battle. But, Rahab believed in the God of Israel. She hid two Israelite spies and helped them escape, asking only that her family be saved when Jericho fell to the Israelites. She staked her life on the fact that the Israelites' God had said He would save and protect His people. She was spared and married into the Hebrew nation. She became the mother of Boaz, who married Ruth, the great-grandmother of King David. Thus Rahab was an ancestor of Jesus Christ.

Think about what it means to live by faith. In both the victory at Jericho and the deliverance of Rahab, we see God act in a way that is contrary to human reasoning. In God's economy, neither might nor strategy accomplishes His purposes, but the faithful obedience of His people does.

God's Faithful Servants

The list goes on to include several people who represent faith during a later period of Jewish history. For the most part, they are judges, prophets, and kings. The first four are judges who served during the gradual expansion of Israelite power in Canaan.

❖ **Gideon** was enlisted into God's service despite his original hesitancy to fully trust God. Nonetheless, emboldened by increased faith, he and an army too small to succeed by natural strength overcame their enemies and returned peace to Israel—all by God's power.

❖ **Barak** commanded the armies of the tribes of Israel and defeated Sisera, commander of the Canaanite chariot force. When the prophetess Deborah, God's chosen leader of Israel, called on Barak to fight Sisera, Barak reacted with uncertainty and then agreed to lead Israel's army into battle—but only if she would go with them.

- **Samson**, a judge of Israel, fought single-handedly against the Philistines many times, but was self-centered and unable to discipline his incredible God-given strength. In his moment of death, he placed his faith solidly in God, praying, *"O Lord GOD, … please strengthen me only this once"* (Judges 16:28). His faith was rewarded, and he is remembered because of how he died rather than how he lived.

- **Jephthah**, another judge of Israel, conquered the Ammonites. Despite a rash vow that he later regretted, Jephthah believed that God, who had given Israel victory in the past, would continue to defend His people. God honored Jephthah for his faith in spite of his mistakes.

- **David**, king of Israel, committed adultery and murder, yet acknowledged his sin and sought God's forgiveness. In addition, he faced his adversaries in battle with utter confidence that God would prevail. David was not perfect, but he pleased God by his trust and readiness to comply with His will.

- The prophet **Samuel** fought against Israel's immorality and idolatry by speaking God's truth. He became a friend and adviser to Saul, the first king of Israel, and later to David.

Several other faithful servants are named, including Daniel, Shadrach, Meshach, Abednego, and Jeremiah. Many people of faith were miraculously delivered, but others suffered and died for their faith. We learn that faith in God does not guarantee safety or comfort in this world.

A Good Report

Despite suffering or victories, these faithful people all lived in hope. None of them received fulfillment of the greatest promise—the coming Messiah. But, they had an abiding confidence that God would one day redeem them. Now the promise has been fulfilled. *"Something better for us"* (11:40) has come through the new covenant established in Christ. Forgiveness of sins is no longer symbolized by animal sacrifice, but is finalized in the death of Jesus. Access to God and fellowship with Him have been attained. Together with us, they receive the promise of perfection in and through Jesus Christ.

Personalize this lesson.

☑ The author has shown us that faith enables God's people to act courageously and accomplish great deeds. We have seen that following Christ does not necessarily result in an easy life. Even giants of faith knew difficulties and trials as well as triumphs. Regardless of our circumstances, God will enable us to live victoriously. God's heroes lived and died by faith. If we would be heroes in His eyes, we, too, must live by faith, so that we *"might rise again to a better life"* (11:35) and receive the promised perfection. Which of the people described in this lesson as heroes of the faith encourage you? What do you learn about them and about God that helps you live with more courage and trust?

Lesson 16

The Value of Hardship
Hebrews 12:1-11

❖ **Hebrews 12:1—Consider the Course of Faith**

1. According to your understanding of chapter 11, who is the great assembly of witnesses who bore witness to their faith (12:1)?

    _____

    _____

2. The first word of 12:1, *"therefore"* is a transition word that calls attention to the text that precedes and follows it. What are the thoughts the author seeks to connect?

    _____

    _____

    _____

3. Whose responsibility is it to *"lay aside"* hindrances and sin? How could this be done?

    _____

    _____

    _____

4. *Endurance* means *determination, continuing steadfastly to the end.* What do the following verses reveal about *"run*[ning] *with endurance the race that is set before us"*?

    a. Hebrews 2:1_____

    _____

    b. Hebrews 10:19-23_____

5. What are some specific *"weights"* that Christians today need to lay aside?

    _____

    _____

    _____

❖ Hebrews 12:2-4—Consider Christ and Be Encouraged

6. According to 12:3, why should we *"consider Him"*?

    _____

    _____

7. To whom does the author refer when he speaks of how Christ *"endured from sinners such hostility against Himself"*? (See Matthew 27:39-44.)

    _____

    _____

8. How can the awareness of Christ's endurance sustain you in times of weariness and discouragement?

    _____

    _____

    _____

9. What idea stated in verse 2 appears in similar form in Psalm 141:8 and Hebrews 3:1? How can you put into practice what these verses talk about?

    _____

    _____

    _____

❖ Hebrews 12:5-6—Consider the Timeless Truth of

Love

10. a. Read Proverbs 3:1-17 (from which Hebrews 5-6 quotes). To whom is the advice directed?

    b. What do you discern as the reason for the instruction?

11. What kind of response to Hebrews 12:5-6 do you think the author hopes to elicit? Explain your answer.

❖ Hebrews 12:7-10—Consider the Meaning of Discipline

12. Why is *respect* the reasonable result of true discipline (12:9)?

13. How is failing to discipline one's children a sign of not loving them well?

14. How would lack of discipline prevent a child of God from sharing in God's holiness?

❖ Hebrews 12:11—Consider the Result of Discipline

15. What images does *"yields ... fruit"* bring to your mind (12:11)?
    From the truth this image conveys, what do you learn about the
    result of discipline?

    _____

    _____

16. Share an example that you have observed of a person exhibiting
    or practicing:

    a. *righteousness*_____

    _____

    _____

    b. *peace*_____

    _____

    _____

17. Why do you think someone who has been "trained by"
    discipline will exhibit these qualities?

    _____

    _____

    _____

Apply what you have learned. Jesus clearly
warned, *"In the world you will have tribulation"*
(John 16:33). How do you respond to hardship?
Are you willing to trust in God's love and goodness, even in
trials? If you submit as a child to God's discipline, hardship
becomes the seed for a harvest of righteousness and peace.
Substituting your name for Israel, read Psalm 131:2-3: *"I
have calmed and quieted my soul, ... like a weaned child is my
soul within me. O Israel, hope in the LORD from this time forth
and forevermore."*

The Value of Hardship
Hebrews 12:1-11

Running the Race

"Therefore" points us back to the heroes of faith in chapter 11, whom the author describes as *"so great a cloud of witnesses."* Some see the witnesses as spectators who look down from heaven like an audience in an amphitheater looks down on participants in an arena. Another view is that, by their steadfastness, these believers have borne witness to the faithfulness of God. Their example inspires perseverance through trials.

"Let us also lay aside every weight" refers to anything that weighs down a runner in a race. Not all that hinders a Christian is sin, but anything that impedes progress should be discarded. What hinders one believer may not affect another. Under the Holy Spirit's guidance, each Christian must decide what to put aside. We must also get rid of *"sin which clings so closely."* Sin is a snare; it can ruin a race.

Finally, the race must be *"run with endurance."* Christians must possess endurance—the determination to keep going even when you want to give up. The word translated *"race"* means *a hard and earnest struggle*. The Christian race is not a sprint; it's a marathon that requires controlled, sustained power that pushes toward its goal.

Think about how even good things could be an obstacle to our spiritual development. The problem is not with the things themselves, but with our attraction to them and the priority we give them. The apostle Paul said, *"I know what it is to be in need, and I know what it is to have plenty. I know how to be brought low, and I know how to abound. In any and every circumstance, I have*

*learned the secret of facing plenty and hunger, abundance and
need. I can do all things through Him who strengthens me"*
(Philippians 4:12-13, NIV). Nothing hindered Paul. He was
intent on running the race. If the Holy Spirit pinpoints
something as a snare in your life, what will you do?

Jesus Christ is the Creator of the course of our race. We look to Jesus
because He is not only the Founder (originator) of the life of faith, but
also He is the perfect model of that life. He fulfilled the will of God and
successfully finished His course of faith. The phrase *"our faith"* implies
that Jesus has begun a work of faith in us that He will see through to
completion.

This is the only place in the book of Hebrews where the author speaks of
the Cross. One aspect of *"the joy"* Jesus anticipated was the restoration
of the glory He had before the Incarnation. *"Endured the cross, despising
the shame"* speaks of the physical and emotional pain that came from
a disgraceful method of death. But Jesus disregarded the pain and
humiliation; they were not worthy of consideration when compared to
the joy of doing His Father's will.

The reward for the Son's obedience is now powerfully stated: He
"is seated." The Resurrection, the Ascension, and the resumption of
eternal authority and glory are all captured in this phrase. The author
is confident in the finished work of Jesus Christ. As Jesus suffered the
misunderstanding and hostility of sinful men, so readers of this epistle
may compare their own lives to Him and *"not grow weary or faint-
hearted"* (12:3).

Enduring Discipline

*"In your struggle against sin you have not yet resisted to the point of shedding
your blood"* (Hebrews 12:4). Those to whom this epistle was originally
written had suffered severe persecution, but they had not yet been called
on to die for their faith. Martyrdom is the fate of only a few, but all God's
people experience discipline.

"My son, do not regard lightly the discipline of the Lord" (12:5) addresses
Christians who have difficulty seeing that God's sovereign grace works
through life's trials as well as its joys. To avoid God's training is to avoid
maturity. Some believers are overwhelmed by the Lord's discipline. They

lose courage under the weight of their troubles. They forget that the God who tests is also the God who loves and helps. He promises that He will not test us beyond what we are able to bear.

"The Lord disciplines the one He loves" (Hebrews 12:6). Instead of being driven to despair by adversity, Christians ought to realize that they are of such value to God that He does all that is necessary to bring them to maturity. Only an unloved child is free of a disciplining hand.

In 12:6, the word *"chastises"* refers to *correction*. The Father works to develop heirs fit for His kingdom. Discipline is evidence of belonging to a family in which all the children have a share. In the ancient world, fathers did not give illegitimate children the same discipline they gave legitimate children. Furthermore, illegitimate children had no claim to inheritance. But the Hebrew readers are legitimate children and need to be thankful for a caring Father's demands and restrictions. Even Christ *"learned obedience through what He suffered"* (Hebrews 5:8).

Discipline is demanding and sometimes painful. It can be compared to surgery or a medical procedure. Medical treatments are often painful, but their purpose of achieving better health is unquestionably good. In a much greater way, the Lord's treatment is designed for the good of those He loves, for in the end *"it yields the peaceful fruit of righteousness"* (12:11). Limited human perspective may make it difficult to perceive the necessity for discipline, but faith sees it as one of God's richest gifts of grace.

While the ultimate purpose of God's discipline is to produce His character in His children, other benefits result as well. First, discipline prevents sin. What seems to be inconvenience or hardship may be God's loving protection. He also disciplines to educate His children for better service. God is concerned for their purity, maturity, and ability to cope with a life of hardship and service. When a person has been tried and tested, has faithfully endured, remaining true to God, that individual will reap a harvest of righteousness and peace.

Personalize this lesson.

✓ While God uses hardship to train us, we must be careful not to see all suffering as punishment; it is often simply a result of living in an imperfect world. We don't need to add guilt to our own or someone else's pain.

When trials come, we may ask God if He has a lesson for us to learn, but sometimes He doesn't make the reason for our pain clear. In times like that a good question to ask God might be, "How do you want me to respond in this hardship?" God can transform us through situations that are overwhelming or relentless. By God's grace and our perseverance, trials can build us up. Therefore we can say: *"We know that for those who love God all things work together for good, for those who are called according to His purpose"* (Romans 8:28).

Lesson 17

Responsibilities of Spiritual Maturity
Hebrews 12:12-29

Memorize God's Word: Hebrews 13:5b-6.

❖ Hebrews 12:12-15—Do This!

1. What two charges are given to believers in 12:14?

   _____

   _____

   _____

2. What two warnings are given in 12:15?

   a. _____

   _____

   b. _____

   _____

3. How can bitterness be avoided?

   _____

   _____

❖ Hebrews 12:16-17—Do Not Do This!

4. According to Genesis 25:29-34, what was Esau's attitude toward his birthright?

   _____

   _____

5. What is *"the right of the firstborn"* as described in
    Deuteronomy 21:15-17?

    _____

    _____

6. What is the warning for us in the account about Esau?

    _____

    _____

    _____

❖ Hebrews 12:18-21—You Are Not Here!

7. Read Exodus 19:12-19 and 20:18-21. What caused a
    common mountain to become so uncommon? (See also
    Deuteronomy 4:10-13.)

    _____

    _____

    _____

    _____

8. What reaction did the Israelites have to this uncommon
    mountain? Why?

    _____

    _____

    _____

❖ Hebrews 12:22-24—You Have Come Here!

9. Read the additional references given with each of the following
    phrases and briefly describe those with whom we share Mount
    Zion.

    a. *"Innumerable angels in festal gathering"* (See Hebrews 1:14;
        Revelation 5:11-12.)

        _____

        _____

   b. *"The assembly of the firstborn who are enrolled in heaven"* (See Luke 10:19-20; Revelation 20:15.)

   c. *"God, the judge of all"* (See Romans 14:10-12; 2 Corinthians 5:10.)

   d. *"The spirits of the righteous made perfect"* (See Philippians 3:8-9, 12; Hebrews 11:39-40.)

   e. *"Jesus, the Mediator of the new covenant"* (See 1 Timothy 2:5; Hebrews 8:6; 9:15.)

❖ Hebrews 12:25-29—Remember These Things!

10. Who are *"they"* in 12:25, and who warned them? (See 3:7-17.)

11. Who warns us, and why is this warning even more significant? (See 1:2; 10:15.)

12. Read Daniel 7:13-14. What specific truths about the kingdom of God are mentioned in these verses?

13. How should *"receiving a kingdom"* (Hebrews 12:28; a present process) affect our attitude and behavior, according to Luke 12:27-34?

_____

_____

_____

14. How should *"receiving a kingdom"* affect our worship, according to Hebrews 12:28?

_____

_____

Apply what you have learned. We encourage a baby's attempts to crawl because the little one's proper development is our goal. So we motivate and instruct, while the baby does the required work. For Christians, there are responsibilities to consider and tasks to master that lead to spiritual maturity and godly character. Our Father encourages, motivates, and coaches. We, however, must make every effort to listen and obey, assisting one another along the way. What "baby steps" do you sense God is encouraging you to make today?

Responsibilities of Spiritual Maturity
Hebrews 12:12-29

Exhortation to Christian Living

Discipline is the path to righteousness and peace, so it benefits
Christians to show courage and resolve in trying times. Using the
familiar language of Isaiah, readers are urged to strengthen their *"weak
hands"* and *"feeble knees"* (Isaiah 35:3). Injured athletes can remain in a
game or return quickly if their lameness is quickly and artfully tended.
In using this illustration, the author exhorts his readers to recognize that
they are not spectators of faith, but participants, and urges them not
to allow anyone to drop out of the race. Smooth, straight paths enable
weaker runners to continue their race without tripping. Verse 13 implies
that by living lives of unswerving faith and obedience, those strong in
faith will maintain a path for those who have been spiritually crippled
through suffering or discouragement. By following this level path, the
lame can be healed.

Another way Christians can preserve the path of faith is to *"Strive for ...
holiness without which no one will see the Lord"* (12:14). Holiness is not
an attained state of perfection (12:10), but is a continuing process in a
person's relationship with God. When believers enter into fellowship
with God, they become sanctified, or set apart for God. As they walk
with Him, more and more they walk like Him. They are continually
cleansed in life and conduct. The purity of character produced by the
Holy Spirit prepares the believer to *"see the Lord"* face-to-face in eternity.

To grow in holiness, Christians must rely on God's grace and help others
also to grasp it. We are warned about the *"root of bitterness,"* which causes
trouble and sin. Deuteronomy 29:18 defines the danger: *"Beware lest
there be among you a man or woman ... whose heart is turning away today*

from the LORD our God ... Beware lest there be among you a root bearing poisonous and bitter fruit."

We must not allow rebellion, and the bitterness it produces, to arise either in our own hearts or among fellow believers. The idea that a person could willingly turn from God's grace reminds our author of Esau. He is considered *"godless"* because he rejected his inheritance as Isaac's firstborn son. The birthright of the firstborn son gave him a position of leadership in the clan and the responsibility of protecting the "covenant status" of Israel. Rejecting this honor and responsibility reveals Esau's shallow appreciation of his place as the firstborn son.

Think about how Esau's appetite was physical rather than spiritual. Devotion to creature comforts more than to God is a widespread form of godlessness even among "respectable Christians." We must not let the subtlety of godlessness weaken our commitment to Jesus Christ. Sensual desires and the lure of material things can dull our appetite for spiritual blessings. Esau set his heart on immediately satisfying his physical desires and forfeited spiritual blessing.

Mount Sinai and Mount Zion

Mount Sinai is the mountain where God spoke to Moses and gave him the Law. Under penalty of death, the people were forbidden to touch the mountain because it was holy. The distance between a holy God and a sinful people was emphasized; even Moses trembled with fear. Upon hearing God's voice, the people begged not to be spoken to again. Their experience was overwhelming, even frightening.

The author contrasts Mount Sinai and Mount Zion. Earthly Mount Zion is where Abraham was prepared to sacrifice Isaac and Solomon built the temple. Jews and many Christians believe the Messiah will establish his rule here. Mount Zion is a more significant place spiritually than Sinai, because of the new covenant. Zion is seen in three ways: as a literal place on earth where God revealed Himself and was worshiped; as a city above, where God dwells; and as the blessedness and enjoyment of life Christians know through Christ.

The heavenly Jerusalem on Mount Zion is an inhabited city. First, there are *"innumerable angels in festal gathering"* (12:22 who worship God (Daniel 7:10), attend believers struggling in life (Hebrews 1:14), and minister goodness and mercy wherever they go. Then the passage speaks of *"the assembly of the firstborn who are enrolled in heaven"* (12:23). The term becomes more understandable when applied to those saints of old (chapter 11) who lived and died in faith.

On Mount Zion, believers may enter God's presence, without fear, because they come in the Savior's righteousness made available by the blood of God's Son. Old Testament saints and all believers who have since died were *"just"* when living for God on earth and have now been made perfect. Verses 22-24 recognize the bond of worship between the angels, the living church, and the *"cloud of witnesses."* Thus, believers stand in a place far superior to that of the Israelites who stood before Mount Sinai in fearful awe. Through Christ, we draw near to God, our judge, with confidence. Jesus' sprinkled blood secures our forgiveness, unlike Abel's shed blood, which cried out for retribution.

An Unshakable Kingdom

Christians must not refuse to hear and obey God's message given through Jesus. To return to the Law from His gospel of grace is to reject a greater truth than that which confronted the Israelites in the wilderness. The Hebrew Christians are repeatedly warned that unbelief is a present danger. The Israelites of the Exodus stand as an example of those who turned from obedience and suffered judgment.

The events at Sinai are linked with the description of the last days. Everything visible and physical will be destroyed; only the eternal, unseen things will remain. Our confidence cannot be shaken because it rests in that which remains. God has prepared *"a new heaven and a new earth"* that includes *"the new Jerusalem."* For God's eternal kingdom, Christians ought to be thankful.

Acceptable worship must be offered with an attitude of reverence and awe, *"for our God is a consuming fire"* (12:29). He, who in absolute holiness descended on Sinai and spoke to His people, is like a refiner's fire that purges all dross and preserves only that which is pure. Our worship should spring from thankful hearts and keep believers from spiritual apathy and its resulting judgment.

Personalize this lesson.

Two words—*judgment* and *mercy*—sum up all the contrasts in Hebrews 12:14-29. This contrast makes us aware of our responsibility to intentionally choose one or the other. As Esau's life demonstrated, it is all too possible to go after temporal goals and miss out on eternal treasures. What eternal treasures do you intentionally seek? Does the "good" ever get in the way of the "best" as you go after this heavenly goal? Ask God to give you an appetite for the things that matter most.

Living Out Our Christian Faith
Hebrews 13

Memorize God's Word: Hebrews 13:15.

❖ Hebrews 13:1-6—What to Do for Others

1. From 13:1-3, identify the people for whom we are to show love and concern.

   _____

   _____

   _____

2. What does the phrase *"as though"* (13:3) imply we should think about while expressing our love and concern?

   _____

   _____

   _____

3. List the moral and practical exhortations found in verses 1-5.

   _____

   _____

   _____

   _____

4. For what reason are believers urged to be content?

   _____

   _____

5. What does the fact that God will never leave nor forsake us allow us to say (and believe) with confidence? Do you have this confidence?

_____

_____

❖ Hebrews 13:7-12—What to Do for Ourselves

6. From 13:7, what must we do as we continue in a life of faith?

_____

_____

7. From verse 9, what must we not do?

_____

_____

8. What comfort do you find in verse 8?

_____

_____

_____

9. When the author speaks of Jesus suffering *"outside the gate"* (13:12), what event and place is he referring to? (See John 19:17-18.)

_____

_____

❖ Hebrews 13:13-17—What to Do Together

10. How does our acceptance of the statement in 13:14 make a difference in obeying the exhortation of verse 13? (See also 12:22-24.)

_____

_____

_____

11. From 13:15-17, what are the acceptable sacrifices that Christians are to offer to God?

    _____

    _____

12. Why do you suppose that some believers find these sacrifices difficult to fulfill?

    _____

    _____

13. What is the main work of a leader according to verses 13:7, 17?

    _____

    _____

14. What do the following verses reveal about genuine Christian leadership?

    a.   Ephesians 3:7-9 _____

        _____

        _____

    b.   1 Peter 5:1-3 _____

        _____

        _____

❖ Hebrews 13:18-21—What to Do Is Demonstrated

15. What does the author ask for in these verses? Why do you think he asked for this?

    _____

    _____

16. In two short verses (13:20-21) at least four things are revealed about God. List as many as you can.

    _____

    _____

17. Which of these is most important or meaningful to you? Why?

_____

_____

18. In 13:15 and 21, the phrases *"through Him"* and *"through Jesus"* are used. What do you think these mean?

_____

_____

_____

❖ Hebrews 13:22-25—P.S.: What to Do for Now

19. What does the very last sentence reveal about the underlying tone or spirit of the letter?

_____

_____

_____

Apply what you have learned. *"Let brotherly love continue"* (Hebrews 13:1). When are we to love? Always. Is it easy? No, it is not. Who do you need God's help to love more consistently? Ask Him to help you. Remember that *"God is able to make all grace abound to you, so that having all sufficiency in all things at all times, you may abound in every good work"* (2 Corinthians 9:8).

Living Out Our Christian Faith
Hebrews 13

General Christian Obligations

"Let brotherly love continue" (13:1). The primary Christian virtue is love. The particular love named here is *philadelphia—brotherly love*. Loving fellow Christians pleases God, demonstrates obedience to Christ's commands, and offers proof of belonging to Him. Jesus said, *"By this all people will know that you are My disciples, if you have love for one another"* (John 13:35). As parents are delighted when they see their children caring for each other, so God is pleased when mutual love exists between His children. Believers are urged to express this love by opening their homes to visitors and being generous.

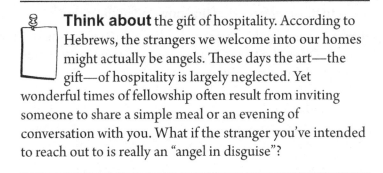

Think about the gift of hospitality. According to Hebrews, the strangers we welcome into our homes might actually be angels. These days the art—the gift—of hospitality is largely neglected. Yet wonderful times of fellowship often result from inviting someone to share a simple meal or an evening of conversation with you. What if the stranger you've intended to reach out to is really an "angel in disguise"?

Brotherly love must also extend to those in prison. Many were in prison because of their faith. *"Those who are mistreated"* may refer to prisoners, but probably includes neighbors or family. Historical records from this period note that Christians visited fellow believers in prison and brought them food and necessities.

How should love affect marriage? Everywhere in Scripture marriage is guarded against harm. In 13:4 its protection is emphasized by one word—*"honor."* The author wants to preserve the rightful place of marriage as an ordinance of God because it is fundamental to social stability. Jews and Christians stood out in 1ˢᵗ-century Roman culture for promoting sexual purity and monogamous commitment. Scripture approves marriage and sex within marriage. Adultery and fornication, however, are impure and are violations of genuine love.

Another false love is the love of money. A materialistic society values money above spiritual, moral, and ethical standards. Therefore, the author recommends that believers *"be content with what you have."* Scriptures are quoted to remind the persecuted Hebrew Christians that God had not forsaken them so they had no need to fear what people might do. No one could rob them of true, lasting possessions.

A Call to Constancy

Their former leaders' commitment to the Lord—the way they lived and perhaps even died—is held up as a pattern to follow. *"Consider the outcome of their way of life, and imitate their faith,"* the author says (13:7). These teachers surely spoke of Jesus Christ, who *"is the same"* for all time. *"Yesterday"* includes offering Himself to God as the atoning sacrifice. *"Today"* He represents and intercedes for His people in God's presence. *"Forever"* includes His work in the consummation of history, and His faithfulness to those who follow Him, now and in the future.

Christ has not changed; therefore the readers should not abandon the truth for strange new doctrines that are contrary to basic New Testament teaching. God's divine power works by grace, through solid teaching, to establish one's heart in the truth, and by grace believers are enabled to stand firm in that truth. The reference to *"foods"* may include the Old Testament practice of priests eating sacrificial animals, the distinction between clean and unclean food, or pagan food ceremonies.

To symbolize the removal of Israel's sin, the bodies of the animals sacrificed on the Day of Atonement were burned outside the camp. Being *"outside the camp"* also symbolized being outside the fellowship of God and His people. To show that Christ's blood sanctified the people and that He bore their sins, He, too, suffered *"outside the gate"* of Jerusalem, on Calvary. The people rejected Him, and God temporarily rejected Him when He became the sin-bearer. His death outside the city walls symbolized that rejection. Followers of Jesus are to *"go to*

Him outside the camp," making a complete break from the old camp of Judaism. They share the disgrace of the Savior's expulsion. No longer should they engage in symbolic cleansing, but instead receive benefits from the living, interceding Savior. Believers are pilgrims and strangers on earth, as they anticipate the eternal city that is coming.

The Christians' Sacrifices—Praise and Service

Just as Christ offered Himself as a better sacrifice than animals, His followers may also offer better sacrifices—sacrifices of praise and service. The sacrifice of thanksgiving for Christians is now a spiritual offering. For the Word, the beauty of creation, and the way He transforms the inner man, adoration should pour from our hearts to His. *"The fruit of lips that acknowledge His name"* describes our audible gratitude that comes before God.

"Do not neglect to do good and to share what you have" (13:16). Out of a proper response to God comes a proper response to people. Ministry to the needs of others was characteristic of the Hebrew Christians and an important part of New Testament doctrine.

Concluding Prayer and Final Exhortations

The author asks his readers to pray for him, then concludes his letter with a prayer for them. The precise content, the poetic form, and the evidence of deep care are striking. God is described as one who creates peace among and in His people. Verse 20 contains the only direct reference to the Resurrection. The covenant sealed by Jesus' blood, unlike the covenant of Law, is eternal.

The phrase *"the great Shepherd of the sheep"* is modeled after Isaiah 63:11. Jesus taught that He is the Good Shepherd who lays down His life for His sheep. The author asks God to prepare the readers to do everything their commitment to Christ requires. Doing God's will is the highest ideal of human life and requires divine grace and power. Glory belongs to both Father and Son *"forever and ever."*

The benediction and prayer is finished; common-sense admonitions follow. Then the letter concludes with a prayer for grace, which is appropriate because grace is its major theme. The author realizes the importance of the doctrine of grace, but his emphasis also reveals an emotional and spiritual experience of the grace he emphasizes.

Personalize this lesson.

✓ The emphasis of Hebrews is on Jesus—who He is, what He has done, and what He is presently doing. What He lived and died to do is completed. Then *"He sat down at the right hand of the Majesty on high"* (1:3). Jesus Christ is still equipping the saints for service and serving as our High Priest. In Hebrews He is uniquely portrayed as our High Priest. He bids us come to Him with confidence to receive mercy and grace; He will always be there for us. How has your view of Jesus as your High Priest changed in this course? Will you regularly go to Him for the forgiveness, grace, and help you need to live for Him more fully? He continually pleads for us in the heavenly sanctuary. So ask Him for what you need! He longs to bring you into full maturity which means joy for both Him and you!

Small Group Leader's Guide

While *Engaging God's Word* is great for personal study, it is generally even more effective and enjoyable when studied with others. Studying with others provides different perspectives and insights, care, prayer support, and fellowship that studying on your own does not. Depending on your personal circumstances, consider studying with your family or spouse, with a friend, in a Sunday school, with a small group at church, work, or in your neighborhood, or in a mentoring relationship.

In a traditional Community Bible Study class, your study would involve a proven four-step method: personal study, a small group discussion facilitated by a trained leader, a lecture covering the passage of Scripture, and a written commentary about the same passage. *Engaging God's Word* provides two of these four steps with the study questions and commentary. When you study with a group, you add another of these—the group discussion. And if you enjoy teaching, you could even provide a modified form of the fourth, the lecture, which in a small group setting might be better termed a wrap-up talk.

Here are some suggestions to help leaders facilitate a successful group study.

1. Decide how long you would like each group meeting to last. For a very basic study, without teaching, time for fellowship, or group prayer, plan on one hour. If you want to allow for fellowship before the meeting starts, add at least 15 minutes. If you plan to give a short teaching, add 15 or 20 minutes. If you also want time for group prayer, add another 10 or 15 minutes. Depending on the components you include for your group, each session will generally last between one and two hours.

2. Set a regular time and place to meet. Meeting in a church classroom or a conference room at work is fine. Meeting in a home is also a good option, and sometimes more relaxed and comfortable.

3. Publicize the study and/or personally invite people to join you.

4. Begin praying for those who have committed to come. Continue to pray for them individually throughout the course of the study.

5. Make sure everyone has his or her own book at least a week before you meet for the first time.

6. Encourage group members to read the first lesson and do the questions before they come to the group meeting.

7. Prepare your own lesson.

8. Prepare your wrap-up talk, if you plan to give one. Here is a simple process for developing a wrap-up talk:

    a. Divide the passage you are studying into two or three divisions. Jot down the verses for each division and describe the content of each with one complete sentence that answers the question, "What is the passage about?"

    b. Decide on the central idea of your wrap-up talk. The central idea is the life-changing principle found in the passage that you believe God wants to implant in the hearts and minds of your group. The central idea answers the question, "What does God want us to learn from this passage?"

    c. Provide one illustration that would make your central idea clear and meaningful to your group. This could be an illustration from your own life, or a story you've read or heard somewhere else.

    d. Suggest one application that would help your group put the central idea into practice.

    e. Choose an aim for your wrap-up talk. The aim answers the question, "What does God want us to do about it?" It encourages specific change in your group's lives, if they choose to respond to the central idea of the passage. Often it takes the form of a question you will ask your group: "Will you, will I choose to … ?"

9. Show up early to the study so you can arrange the room, set up the refreshments (if you are serving any), and welcome people as they arrive.

10. Whether your meeting includes a fellowship time or not, begin the discussion time promptly each week. People appreciate it when you respect their time. Transition into the discussion with prayer, inviting God to guide the discussion time and minister personally to each person present.

11. Model enthusiasm to the group. Let them know how excited you are about what you are learning—and your eagerness to hear what God is teaching them.

12. As you lead through the questions, encourage everyone to participate, but don't force anyone. If one or two people tend to dominate the discussion, encourage quieter ones to participate by saying something like, "Let's hear from someone who hasn't shared yet." Resist the urge to teach during discussion time. This time is for your group to share what they have been discovering.

13. Try to allow time after the questions have been discussed to talk about the "Apply what you have learned," "Think about" and "Personalize this lesson" sections. Encourage your group members in their efforts to partner with God in allowing Him to transform their lives.

14. Transition into the wrap-up talk, if you are doing one (see number 8).

15. Close in prayer. If you have structured your group to allow time for prayer, invite group members to pray for themselves and one another, especially focusing on the areas of growth they would like to see in their lives as a result of their study. If you have not allowed time for group prayer, you as leader can close this time.

16. Before your group finishes their final lesson, start praying and planning for what your next *Engaging God's Word* study will be.

COMMUNITY
BIBLE STUDY

Million+ people are engaging with God and His Word through CBS

Community Bible Study (CBS) is a global, interdenominational Bible study ministry offering a wide range of courses exploring various books of the Bible in both written and spoken formats, for all ages. Currently available in more than 85 languages, CBS Bible studies impact lives across more than 110 countries worldwide.

Since 1975, CBS has served as a conduit for the transformative power of God's Word; our participants study the Bible together in diverse settings, such as churches, prisons, schools, refugee camps, homes, coffee shops, and on the Internet. CBS is a participation-based ministry with trained leaders who foster in-depth, holistic engagement with God's Word within the context of a caring community, both in person and online.

The vision of Community Bible Study is, "Transformed Lives Through the Word of God."

The mission of Community Bible Study is, "To make disciples of the Lord Jesus Christ in our communities through caring, in-depth Bible Study, available to all."

CBS makes every effort to stand in the center of mainstream historic Christianity, concentrating on the essentials of the Christian faith rather than denominational distinctives. CBS respects different theological views, preferring to focus on helping people know God through His Word, grow deeper in their relationship with Jesus, and be transformed into His likeness.

Are you ready to go deeper in God's Word?

We would love to have you join us for an in-person or online CBS group. Scan the QR code to find a group.

For more information call 1-719-955-7777 or email info@communitybiblestudy.org.

Engage Bible Studies are available from Amazon and fine bookstores near you.

Scan the QR code to see all the available titles.

12109700R00089